The Teacher's Guidebook
to
Piano Literature

A Recommended Listing of Graded Repertoire for Elementary, Intermediate and Lower Advanced Students

First Edition

By

Alice M. Kern
and
Helen M. Titus
University of Michigan
Ann Arbor, Michigan

Revised By
Alice M. Kern

Edwards Brothers, Inc.
Ann Arbor, Michigan

First Edition, Second Printing: April 1955
First Edition, Third Printing: September 1955
First Edition, Fourth Printing: January 1958
First Edition, Fifth Printing: September 1961
Revised Edition, August 1964

Library of Congress Catalog Card Number: 64-24787

PREFACE TO REVISED EDITION

The first edition of The Teacher's Guidebook To Piano Literature has been completely revised to include changes in publishers, numerous new collections of piano music which have been made available in the past few years, and approximately four hundred and thirty-five additional compositions. Any collections or individual compositions no longer available have been omitted from this new edition.

The graded listing, the method of examination and selection of materials and the same classification of the music by centuries have been retained. For this reason, the Foreword written by Alice Kern and Helen Titus can still serve for this revised edition.

Alice M. Kern

Ann Arbor, Michigan
August, 1964

FOREWORD

This book is primarily designed for the convenience of teachers of piano. It lists nearly four thousand available compositions which have been selected particularly for the elementary and intermediate student.

The graded listing of materials presented is the result of many years of study and examination of music from the teacher's point of view. It grew out of a course in "Methods and Materials for Piano Teachers" which we have taught for some time at the University of Michigan. We received further encouragement in our project from discussions and correspondence with colleagues throughout the country, from conferences and workshops with various organizations of piano teachers, and from many young inexperienced teachers who have sought our advice from time to time. These teachers have all requested a concrete listing of materials which would best suit their needs. We have tried to meet these needs by listing each composition according to grade level and according to an arbitrary chronological classification, so that it will facilitate the planning of a well balanced repertoire. We have mentioned various collections in which each composition may be found, giving names of publishers and indicating which compositions are also published separately.

Our procedure has been the careful examination of each work listed, with reference to its general grade level and its merit in the field of piano literature. Each work has been studied, analyzed, and evaluated for its suitability in a recommended list. Although we realize the excellent teaching value of many other publications, we have limited the list to composers whose general output has seemed significant. Methods for beginners have not been included, nor have the standard exercises.

We have used the more flexible divisions of grade levels indicated by Lower Elementary, Upper Elementary, Intermediate, and Lower Advanced. Because of the uneven musical and technical development of many students, the standards of accomplishment at the end of a given period will be different with each student. It is suggested that the teacher also be flexible in the use of materials from the graded lists.

Our arbitrary breakdown of the classification of the music by centuries may arouse controversy. Because of the varied styles of composers of a specific period, it is sometimes difficult to decide where to place these composers, historically speaking. For that reason, we have included after each composer's name his birth and death dates, as a matter of convenience. We have arbitrarily included the works of composers who died before 1825 under the listings of the sixteenth, seventeenth and eighteenth centuries; later composers who died before 1910 under the nineteenth century and composers who are still living or who died after 1910 under the twentieth century.

We hope that the further study of the music recommended in this book will provide as much stimulation and be of as much practical value as it has been to us.

Alice M. Kern

Helen M. Titus

Ann Arbor, Michigan
April, 1954

iv

CONTENTS

SECTION I

LOWER ELEMENTARY

GRADES I AND II

MUSIC OF THE SIXTEENTH, SEVENTEENTH
AND EIGHTEENTH CENTURIES

Composer	Title	Publisher	Volume or Collection
AGINCOURT, F. de (1684-1757)	Le Colin Maillard	BH	Airs and Dances, Bk. I
BACH, C. P. E. (1714-1788)	Allegretto in F	C	Eighteenth Century Music, Vol. I (No. 4)
	Allegro di molto	K	The Direct Path (Hermann)
	March in C	O	Piano Music for Young Wolfgang
	Minuet in F	C	Eighteenth Century Music, Vol. I
	Minuet in F Minor	C	Eighteenth Century Music, Vol. I
BACH, J. C. F. (1732-1795)	Allegro in C	Sch	Clavierstücke für Anfänger
	Schwaebisch in D	Sch	Clavierstücke für Anfänger
	Minuet I in D	C Sch	Eighteenth Century Music, Vol. I Menuetten fürs Clavier, (Kreutz)
	Minuet II in D	C Sch	Eighteenth Century Music, Vol. I Menuetten fürs Clavier, (Kreutz)
BACH, J. S. (1685-1750)	Aria di Giovannini	K BMC	Little Notebook for Anna Magdalena Bach Bach for Early Grades, Bk. I
	Aria, "So oft ich meine Tobackspfeife" (When My Pipe I Smoke)	K BMC	Little Notebook for Anna Magdalena Bach Bach for Early Grades, Bk. I (No. 5)
	Aria in F	K BMC	Little Notebook for Anna Magdalena Bach Bach for Early Grades, Bk. I
	Aria, "Warum betrübst du dich"	K GS	Little Notebook for Anna Magdalena Bach (pg. 102) Master Series for the Young (pg. 4)
	Chorale, "Wie wohl ist mir"	K BMC	Little Notebook for Anna Magdalena Bach Bach for Early Grades, Bk. I
	Chorale in E Minor	BMC	Bach for Early Grades, Bk. I
	Chorale, "Schaff's mit mir, Gott" (Do as Thou willst with me, O Lord)	BMC	Bach for Early Grades, Bk. I
	Hymn in F Major (I Rest in Thy Love)	GS He	Master Series for the Young A Little Treasury of Classics, Bk. I (Lambert)
	Little Choral	S	Le Petit Classique (Morhange-Motchane)
	Menuet in D Minor	K K GS	Little Notebook for Anna Magdalena Bach The First Bach Book First Lessons in Bach, Bk. I (Carroll)

Composer	Title	Publisher	Volume or Collection
BACH, J. S. (cont.)		CF	Bach First Lessons, Bk. I (Carroll)
		BMC	Bach for Early Grades, Bk. I
		I	The Little Music Book of Anna Magdalena Bach
		P	Notenbuch der Anna Magdalena Bach (Sauer)
	Menuet in G Minor	K	Little Notebook for Anna Magdalena Bach
		K	The First Bach Book
		GS	First Lessons in Bach, Bk. I (Carroll) (No. 2)
		CF	Bach First Lessons, Bk. I (No. 2)
		BMC	Bach for Early Grades, Bk. I (No. 8)
		GS	Master Series for the Young
		I	The Little Music Book of Anna Magdalena Bach
		P	Notenbuch der Anna Magdalena Bach (Sauer)
		PP	Hundred Best Short Classics, Bk. I
		K	Bach and His Contemporaries
	Two Menuets in G	K	Little Notebook for Anna Magdalena Bach
		K	The First Bach Book
		GS	First Lessons in Bach, Bk. I (Carroll)
		CF	Bach, First Lessons, Bk. I (Carroll)
		BMC	Bach for Early Grades, Bk. I
		GS	Master Series for the Young
		I	The Little Music Book of Anna Magdalena Bach
		P	Notenbuch der Anna Magdalena Bach (Sauer)
		PP	Hundred Best Short Classics, Bk. I
	Minuet in G	GS	First Lessons in Bach, Bk. I, (Carroll) (No. 7)
		BH	From Ancient to Modern (Rowley)
		K	Bach and His Contemporaries
		CF	Bach, First Lessons, Bk. I (Carroll) (No. 1)
		Su	Piano Literature of the 17th, 18th, and 19th Centuries, Bk. 2 (Clark)
	Minuets in G Minor	GS	First Lessons in Bach, Bk. I (Carroll) (Nos. 6 and 8)
		CF	Bach First Lessons, Bk. I (Nos. 6 and 8)
		Su	Piano Literature of the 17th, 18th and 19th Centuries, Bk. 2 (Clark)
	(Minuet I)	Co	The Solo Book, Vol. III (Zeetlin and Goldberger)
	Musette in D	K	Little Notebook for Anna Magdalena Bach
		K	The First Bach Book
		GS	First Lessons in Bach, Bk. I (Carroll)
		CF	Bach First Lessons, Bk. I (Carroll)
		BMC	Bach for Early Grades, Bk. I
		GS	Master Series for the Young
		I	The Little Music Book of Anna Magdalena Bach

Composer	Title	Publisher	Volume or Collection
BACH, J. S. (cont.)	Musette in D	P	Notenbuch der Anna Magdalena Bach (Sauer)
		CF	Road to Piano Artistry, Vol. II (Scionti)
		Su	Piano Literature of the 17th, 18th and 19th Centuries, Bk. 2 (Clark)
	Musette in G Major (from English Suite III)	K	English Suites
		PP	Hundred Best Short Classics, Bk. II
		K	The First Bach Book
		CF	Bach First Lessons, Bk. I (Carroll)
		GS	First Lessons in Bach, Bk. I (Carroll)
	Polonaise in G Minor	K	Little Notebook for Anna Magdalena Bach
		K	The First Bach Book
		BMC	Bach for Early Grades, Bk. I
		GS	Master Series for the Young (pg. 9)
		P	Notenbuch der Anna Magdalena Bach (Sauer) (pg. 10)
BACH, W. F. (1710-1784)	Minuet in E-flat	C	Eighteenth Century Music, Vol. I
BLOW, J. (1649-1708)	Song Tune	H	Contemporaries of Purcell
CLARK, J. (1670-1707)	Minuet in G	H	Contemporaries of Purcell
	Trumpet Tune	BH	From Ancient to Modern (Rowley)
CORELLI, A. (1653-1713)	Allegro Vivace	BH	Airs and Dances, Bk. II (Dorolle)
	Sarabande in D Minor	P	Sonatinen Vorstufe, Vol. II
COUPERIN, F. (1668-1733)	Air in C	U	Old Masters for Young Pianists, Bk. I (Kuranda)
		U	Grosse Meister für Kleine Hände, Bk. I (Kuranda)
	Carnival	He	A Little Treasury of Classics, Bk. I (Lambert)
	Merry Fair Music	U	Old Masters for Young Pianists, Bk. I (Kuranda)
		U	Grosse Meister für Kleine Hände, Bk. I (Kuranda)
	The Tambourines	He	A Little Treasury of Classics, Bk. I (Lambert)
DANDRIEU, de (1684-1740)	Dance at the Fair	He	A Little Treasury of Classics, Bk. I (Lambert)
DAQUIN, C. (1694-1772)	Noël	BH	Airs and Dances, Bk. I (Dorolle)
	Rigaudon	S	Le Petit Classique (Morhange-Motchane)
DIEUPART, C. (----- 1740)	Menuett in A	P	Contemporaries of Telemann

Composer	Title	Publisher	Volume or Collection

DUNCOMBE, W.
(?)
	Sonatina in C
	  Vivace
	  Trumpet Menuet
	  Hunting Jig
		BH	Early English Sonatinas (Rowley)

	Vivace (Sonatina in C)	He	Little Treasury of Sonatinas, Bk. I
FIOCCO, J. H. (1690- ?)	La Légère	BH	Airs and Dances, Bk. I (Dorolle)

FISCHER, J. K. F.
(1650-1746)
	From "The Notebook"
	  Gavotte in G
	  Menuet in D
	  Menuet in D Minor
	  Menuet in F
	  Menuet in G
	  Menuet in G
	  Menuet in G
		Sch	Notebook of Johann Kasper
			    Ferd. Fischer
			(No. 8)
			(No. 3)
			(No. 12)
			(No. 1)
			(No. 2)
			(No. 6)

	Präludium in C	K	The Direct Path (Hermann)
GRAUPNER, C. (1683-1760)	Menuett in C Menuett in G	P	Contemporaries of Telemann
HANDEL, G. F. (1685-1759)	Menuett in G	He	A Little Treasury of Classics, Bk. I (Lambert)

	Little Dances
	  Gavotte in D
	  Gavotte in G Minor
	  Menuett in A Minor
	  Menuett in B-flat
	  Menuett in F
	  Menuett in F
	  Menuett in G
	  Menuett in G Minor
	  Passepied in A
	  Passepied in C
	  Sarabande in F
	  Sarabande in F
	  Zwei Menuetto in G
	    Minor
		Sch	Twenty Little Dances (Frey)
			(No. 11)
			(No. 3)
			(No. 10)
			(No. 1)
			(No. 6)
			(No. 17)
			(No. 4)
			(No. 13)
			(No. 5)
			(No. 9)
			(No. 2)
			(No. 8)
			(No. 7)

	Minuet in F	Su	Piano Literature of the 17th, 18th, and 19th Centuries, Bk. 5a (Clark)
HAYDN, J. (1732-1809)	Allegretto in B-flat	U	Little Dances for Young Folk (No. 5)
	Allegretto in F	U CF	Little Dances for Young Folk (No. 8) Road to Piano Artistry, Vol. I (Scionti)
	(Tendrement) (Little Dance)	S BH	Le Petit Classique (Morhange-Motchane) From Ancient to Modern (Rowley)
	Allegro Giocosco in C	U	Little Dances for Young Folk (No. 7)
	Allegro Maestoso	U	Little Dances for Young Folk (No. 12)
	Allegro Risoluto	U	Little Dances for Young Folk (No. 6)

Composer	Title	Publisher	Volume or Collection
HAYDN, J. (cont.)	Allegro Vivace	U	Little Dances for Young Folk (No. 10)
	Country Dance in D	He	A Little Treasury of Classics, Bk. II (Lambert)
	Le bonne humeur	S	Le Petit Classique (Morhange-Motchane)
	Etude in G	CF	Road to Piano Artistry, Vol. I (Scionti)
	German Dance	He	A Little Treasury of Classics, Bk. II (Lambert)
	Laendler	S	Le Petit Classique (Morhange-Motchane)
	Moderato in A	U	Little Dances for Young Folk (No. 11)
	Moderato in G	U	Little Dances for Young Folk (No. 4)
	Rustic Dance	S	Le Petit Classique (Morhange-Motchane)
	Ten German Dances	K	German Dances
	Three German Dances	Su	Piano Literature of the 17th, 18th and 19th Centuries, Bk. 3 (Clark)
HILLER, J. A. (1728-1804)	Minuetto in A	Sch	Simple Short Piano Pieces (Kreutz) (No. 2a)
	Minuetto in F	Sch	Simple Short Piano Pieces (No. 5)
HOOK, J. (1746-1827)	Hunting Song	BH	Old English Worthies (Rowley)
KIRNBERGER, J. P. (1721-1783)	Minuet in E minor	Su	Kirnberger Collection (Jonas)
	Minuet Pastorale	Su	Kirnberger Collection (Jonas)
	Minuetto in C	Sch	Clavierstücke für Anfänger
	Minuetto in G		
KREBS, J. (1713-1780)	Harlequinade	Co	The Solo Book, Vol. 3 (Zeetlin and Goldberger)
KUHNAU, J. (1660-1722)	Sarabande in F	GS	Introduction to Piano Classics, Vol. II (Mirovitch)
LÖHLEIN, G. S. (1727-1782)	Balletto	Sch	Clavierstücke für Anfänger
MOURET, J. J. (1682-1735)	La Montagnarde	BH	Airs and Dances, Bk. I (Dorolle)
MOZART, L. (1719-1785)	Angloise	Sch	Notebook for Wolfgang (No. 19)
	Aria	Sch	Notebook for Wolfgang (No. 21)
	Bourrée in E Minor	Sch	Notebook for Wolfgang (No. 11)
	Bourrée in D Minor	O	Piano Music for Young Wolfgang (No. 6)
	Burlesque	Sch	Notebook for Wolfgang (No. 3)
		O	Piano Music for Young Wolfgang (No. 5)

Composer	Title	Publisher	Volume or Collection
MOZART, L. (cont.)		He	A Little Treasury of Classics, Bk. II (Lambert)
	Entrée	Sch	Notebook for Wolfgang (No. 10)
		O	Piano Music for Young Wolfgang (No. 5)
	Eight Minuetts	Sch	Notebook for Nannerl Mozart
		He	Nannerl Mozart's Piano Book (Kreutzer)
	Fantasia in D	O	Piano Music for Young Wolfgang (No. 9)
	March in F	Sch	Notebook for Nannerl Mozart
		He	Nannerl Mozart's Piano Book (Kreutzer)
		S	Le Petit Classique (Morhange-Motchane)
	Menuets in C	Sch	Notebook for Wolfgang (Nos. 1, 8, 16)
	Menuets in D	Sch	Notebook for Wolfgang (Nos. 7, 13)
	Menuets in D Minor	O	Piano Music for Young Wolfgang (Nos. 2, 4)
	Menuet in F	Sch	Notebook for Nannerl Mozart (No. 12)
		He	Nannerl Mozart's Piano Book (Kreutzer)
	Musette in C	Sch	Notebook for Wolfgang (No. 14)
		O	Piano Music for Young Wolfgang (No. 8)
	Polonaise in C	O	Piano Music for Young Wolfgang (No. 1)
	Polonaise in C	Sch	Notebook for Wolfgang (No. 6)
	Polonaise in D	Sch	Notebook for Wolfgang (No. 4)
	Sarabande in D	Sch	Notebook for Wolfgang (No. 17)
	Schwaben-Tanz	Sch	Notebook for Wolfgang (No. 12)
		Su	Piano Literature of the 17th, 18th and 19th Centuries, Bk. 4a (Clark)
	Tempo di Marcia	O	Piano Music for Young Wolfgang (No. 12)
	Waldhorn-Stück	Sch	Notebook for Wolfgang (No. 9)
MOZART, W. (1756-1791)	Adagio in D	Sch	A Little Book of Easy Dances (Rehberg)
	Air in A-flat	Sch	The Young Mozart
		H	Easiest Original Pieces
	(Chantons ensemble)	S	Le Petit Classique (Morhange-Motchane)
	Air in E-flat (Trio of Minuet I)	Sch	The Young Mozart
		H	Easiest Original Pieces
	Allegretto in F	Sch	The Young Mozart
	Allegro in B-flat (K 3)	Sch	The Young Mozart
		BMC	Mozart's First Five Compositions
		GS	Master Series for the Young
		He	A Treasury of Easy Classics (Abrams)
		Su	Piano Literature of the 17th, 18th and 19th Centuries, Bk. 2 (Clark)
		K	Mozart, Easy Compositions for Piano
		He	A Treasury of Easy Classics (Abrams)
	(Air tendre)	S	Le Petit Classique (Morhange-Motchane)

Composer	Title	Publisher	Volume or Collection
MOZART, W. (cont.)	Andante in E-flat	Sch	The Young Mozart
		K	Mozart, Easy Compositions for Piano (No. 8)
	Contredance in A (K 15L)	Co	The Classic Dances (Goldberger)
		H	Easiest Original Pieces (No. 2)
	Kontretanz in G (K 15e)	Sch	The Young Mozart
		Co	The Classic Dances (Goldberger)
	Menuet in C (Les premiers pas)	BH	Airs and Dances, Bk. I (Dorolle)
		S	Le Petit Classique (Morhange-Motchane)
	Menuett and Trio ("Air"—Trio only) (Trio only)	H	Easiest Original Pieces
		K	Mozart, Easy Compositions for Piano
		Sch	The Young Mozart
	Menuett in C (K 6)	Sch	Notebook for Nannerl Mozart (pg. 24)
	Menuett in D (K 7) (Confidence)	Sch	Notebook for Nannerl Mozart
		S	Le Petit Classique (Morhange-Motchane)
	Menuett in F (K 2)	BMC	Mozart, First Five Compositions
		Sch	The Young Mozart
		K	Mozart, Easy Compositions for Piano
		H	Easiest Original Pieces
		PP	Hundred Best Short Classics, Bk. I
		K	Easy Compositions by Mozart and Beethoven
		GS	Master Series for the Young
		Co	The Classic Dances (Goldberger)
		Su	Piano Literature of the 17th, 18th and 19th Centuries, Bk. 2 (Clark)
		S	Le Petit Classique
		WR	Rediscovered Classics, Bk. I (Henderson)
	Menuett in F (K 6)	Sch	Notebook for Nannerl Mozart
		Co	The Solo Book, Vol. III (Zeetlin and Goldberger)
		He	Nannerl Mozart's Piano Book
	Menuett in F	K	Mozart, Easy Compositions For Piano
		Sch	The Young Mozart (pg. 11)
		Co	The Classic Dances (Goldberger)
	(Dansons un Menuet)	S	Le Petit Classique (Morhange-Motchane)
	Menuett in F (K 5)	He	A Treasury of Easy Classics (Abrams)
		K	Mozart, Easy Compositions for Piano (No. 7)
		BMC	Mozart, First Five Compositions
		Sch	The Young Mozart (pg. 16)
		Co	The Classic Dances (Goldberger)
	Menuett in G (K 1)	K	Easy Compositions by Mozart and Beethoven
		GS	Master Series for the Young
		K	Mozart, Easy Compositions for Piano
		BMC	Mozart, First Five Compositions
		Su	Piano Literature of the 17th, 18th and 19th Centuries, Bk. 3 (Clark)

Composer	Title	Publisher	Volume or Collection
MOZART, W. (cont.)		Sch	The Young Mozart
		Co	The Classic Dances (Goldberger)
	Minuet in G (K 15c)	Co	The Classic Dances (Goldberger)
	Passepied	Sch	A Little Book of Easy Dances (Rehberg)
MÜLLER, A. (1767-1817)	Allegro-Stücke	P	Sonatinen Vorstufe, Vol. I (No. 4)
	Andante-Stücke		(No. 1)
	Andantino		(No. 5)
	Scherzo		(No. 6)
NEEFE, C. G. (1748-1798)	Allegretto in C	Sch	Clavierstücke für Anfänger
	Minuetto in G		
	Scherzo in E-flat		
NICHELMANN, C. (1717-1762)	Menuetto I in G	Sch	Clavierstücke für Anfänger
	Menuetto II in G Minor		
PURCELL, D. (1660-1717)	Hornpipe in D Minor	H	Contemporaries of Purcell
PURCELL, H. (1658-1695)	Ayre in D Minor	He	A Little Treasury of Classics, Bk. I (Lambert)
		PP	The Fredrick Moore Collection Published Separately
		S	Le Petit Classique (Morhange-Motchane)
	Irish Tune	BMC	Purcell-Arne Album
	March in C, No. 1		
	March in C, No. 9 (From Suite 5)		
	Menuet in F	BH	Airs and Dances, Bk. I
	Prelude in G (From Suite I)	A	Beringer's School of Easy Classics: Old English and French Masters
		BMC	Purcell-Arne Album
		He	A Little Treasury of Classics, Bk. III (Lambert)
	Prelude	Co	The Solo Book, Vol. III (Zeetlin and Goldberger)
	Scotch Tune	BMC	Purcell-Arne Album
	Song Tune		
	Sicilienne	S	Le Petit Classique (Morhange-Motchane)
	Trumpet Tune, No. 1	GS	Introduction to Piano Classics, Vol. I (Mirovitch)
	(Fanfare)	S	Le Petit Classique (Morhange-Motchane)
RAMEAU, J. P. (1683-1764)	Rigaudon	S	Le Petit Classique (Morhange-Motchane)

Composer	Title	Publisher	Volume or Collection

REINECKE, K.
(1774-1820)
	Serenade, Op. 183
	  Gavotte
	  Lied
	  Praeludium
		P	Sonatinen Vorstufe, Vol. 1

ROUSSEAU, J. (1712-1778)	Air sur sol-la-si	S	Le Petit Classique (Morhange-Motchane)
	Le Devin du Village	BH	Airs and Dances, Bk. I (Dorolle)

SCARLATTI, A.
(1659-1725)
	Aria (From Toccata
	  Seconda)
		GS	Introduction to Piano Classics, Vol. I
			  (Mirovitch)

	Minuet in E Minor
	  (From Toccata Quarta)
		GS	Introduction to Piano Classics, Vol. I
			  (Mirovitch)

		K	Easy Pieces from Old Italian Masters
SCHALE, C. F. (1713-1800)	Minuetto I in C	Sch	Clavierstücke für Anfänger
	Minuetto II in C Minor		
	Polonaise in C		
SOLER, A. (1729-1783)	Allegretto in D Minor	BH	Airs and Dances, Bk. I (Dorolle)
TÜRK, D. G. (TUERK) (1750-1813)	Arioso in F	Sch	Clavierstücke für Anfänger

	Eighteen Selected Pieces
	  5. Syncopation
	  6. Swinging
	  7. The Trill
	  8. A Ballet Step
	  9. Ties
	  10. Frolic
	  11. A Grey Cloud
	  12. A Song-Story
	  13. Waltz
	  14. Gavotte
	  15. At Evening
	  16. Neighbors
	  17. Miniature Rondo
	  18. The Horn with Echo
	  19. Gentleness
	  20. The Chase
	  21. A Regal Dance
	  22. Joke
	    (Scherzando)
		K
		
		GS
			Türk, 49 Pieces for Beginners at the
			  Piano
			
			Early Classics for the Piano (Mirovitch)

	Four Pieces for Beginners
	  1. Minuet
	  2. March
	  3. Two Melodies
	  4. The Ladder
		He
		
		K
			A Little Treasury of Classics, Bk. I
			  (Lambert)
			Türk, 49 Pieces for Beginners

	From "Kleine Handstücke" Nos. 5-22 No. 48	NV	Türk: Kleine Handstücke

Composer	Title	Publisher	Volume or Collection
UHDE, J. O. (1725-1766)	Minuetto in B-flat	Sch	Clavierstücke für Anfänger
	Minuetto in G		
WAGENSEIL, G. (1715-1777)	Menuett in C	U	Grosse Meister für kleine Hände, Bk. 2
	Scherzo	Sch	Notebook for Nannerl Mozart
	(Scherzo in C)	He	Nannerl Mozart's Piano Book
WITTHAUER, J. G. (1750-1802)	Allegretto in F	Sch	Clavierstücke für Anfänger (No. 3)
	Allegretto in F		(No. 8)
	Gavotte		(No. 1)
YOUNG, A. (18th cen.)	The Prince's March	BH	Old English Worthies (Rowley)

MUSIC OF THE NINETEENTH CENTURY

Composer	Title	Publisher	Volume or Collection
ANDRÉ, J. A. (1832-1882)	Bagatelle	Co	The Solo Book, Vol. III (Zeetlin and Goldberger)
	Sonatine in C	He	A Little Treasury of Sonatinas, Bk. I (Lambert)
BEETHOVEN, L. van (1770-1827)	Ecossaise in E flat	Co	The Solo Book, Vol. III (Zeetlin and Goldberger)
		Sch	Kleine Tänze (Frey)
	(Schottish)	He	A Treasury of Easy Classics (Abrams)
		PP	Hundred Best Short Classics, Bk. I
		S	Le Petit Classique (Morhange-Motchane)
		Su	Piano Literature of the 17th, 18th and 19th Centuries, Bk. 4b (Clark)
	Ecossaise in G	Sch	Kleine Tänze (Frey) (No. 2)
		CF	Road to Piano Artistry, Vol. 1 (Scionti)
	German Dance in D, No. 5	S	Le Petit Classique (Morhange-Motchane)
	Les Paysans	S	Le Petit Classique (Morhange-Motchane)
	Little Russian Dance	Su	Piano Literature of the 17th, 18th and 19th Centuries, Bk. 2, (Clark)
	Promenade	S	Le Petit Classique (Morhange-Motchane)
	Six German Dances	Su	Piano Literature of the 17th, 18th and 19th Centuries, Bk. 2 (Clark)
	Two Country Dances	Sch	Kleine Tänze (Frey) (No. 1)
		Su	Piano Literature of the 17th, 18th and 19th Centuries, Bk. 4b (Clark)
BERTINI, D. (1798-1876)	Menuetto in G (From "Petits Morceaux")	P	Sonatinen Vorstufe, Vol. II (No. 37)
BURGMÜLLER, F. (1810-1836)	Allegretto	Co	The Solo Book, Vol. III (Zeetlin and Goldberger)
	Ave Maria	GS	Twenty-five Easy and Progressive Studies, Op. 100
		He	
		Wo	
		P	
		CF	Road to Piano Artistry, Vol. II (Scionti)
	Ballade	GS	Twenty-five Easy and Progressive Studies, Op. 100
		He	
		Wo	
		P	

13

Composer	Title	Publisher	Volume or Collection
BURGMÜLLER, F. (cont.)		He	A Little Treasury of Classics, Bk. III (Lambert)
	Barcarolle	GS	Twenty-five Easy and Progressive Studies, Op. 100
		He	
		P	
		Wo	
	Consolation		
	Douce Plainte (Tender Grieving)		
	Inquietude		
	Innocence		
	L'Arabesque		
	La Babillarde (The Chatterbox)		
	La Bergeronnette (The Wagtail)		
	La Chasse (The Chase)		
	La Gracieuse (Grace)		
	La Tarantelle		
	Le Courant limpide (The Limpid Stream)		
	L'Harmonie des Anges (Harmony of the Angels)	GS	Twenty-five Easy and Progressive Studies, Op. 100
		P	
		He	
		Wo	
		CF	Road to Piano Artistry, Vol. II (Scionti)
	L'Hirondelle (The Swallow)	GS	Twenty-five Easy and Progressive Studies, Op. 100
		P	
		He	
		Wo	
	Progrés		
	Tendre Fleur (Tender Blossom)		
CLEMENTI, M. (1752-1832)	Spiritoso, From Sonatina Op. 36, No. 1	GS	Clementi: Six Sonatinas, Op. 36
		P	
		GS	Album of Sonatinas
		P	Sonatinen Album, Vol. I
		GS	Thirty-two Sonatinas and Rondos
		Su	Piano Literature of the 17th, 18th and 19th Centuries, Bk. 3 (Clark)
	Un poco Adagio, From Sonatina Op. 36, No. 3	GS	Thirty-two Sonatinas and Rondos
		P	Sonatinen Album, Vol. I
		GS	Album of Sonatinas

Composer	Title	Publisher	Volume or Collection
CLEMENTI, M. (cont.)		GS P	Clementi: Six Sonatinas, Op. 36
CONCONE, G. (1810-1861)	Springtime, Op. 24	WR	Rediscovered Classics, Bk. I (Henderson)
GURLITT, C. (1820-1901)	From "Album Leaves," Op. 101 1. March 3. The Sunshiny Morning 4. Northern Strains 5. By the Spring 6. Slumber Song 7. Lament 8. The Fair 9. Turkish March 10. Song without Words 11. Waltz 12. The Little Wanderer 13. Grandfather's Birth-day 16. Scherzo 17. Free Fancies 18. Sunday 19. Hunting Song 20. Salto Mortale	GS	Album Leaves for the Young, Op. 101
	A Little Dance, Op. 130, No. 11	GS	Selected Piano Solos by Romantic Composers, Bk. I
	From, "By The Fireside", Op. 183, Nos. 1, 2, 6, 7, 8	BH	By The Fireside, Op. 183
	March of the Tin Soldiers, Op. 130, No. 6	GS	Selected Piano Solos by Romantic Composers, Bk. 1
	Melodious Studies, Op. 131 1. Cheerily, Oh! 2. Undaunted 3. Joyous and Mirthful 5. Through Mountain and Valley 6. Scherzo	GS	Twenty-four Melodious Studies, Op. 131
	Prayer, Op. 130, No. 4	GS	Selected Piano Solos by Romantic Composers, Bk. I
	Serious Moments, Op. 130, No. 23		
	The Fair, Op. 101, No. 8		
	Waltz, Op. 101, No. 11		
HASSLINGER, K. (1816-1868)	Sonatine in C	He	Little Treasury of Sonatinas, Bk. I

Composer	Title	Publisher	Volume or Collection
HELLER, S. (1813-1888)	L'Avalanche, Op. 45, No. 2	R P GS GS	Twenty-five Studies for Piano, Op. 45 Fifty Selected Studies, No. 16 Published Separately
	The Coquette, Op. 47, No. 3	R P GS	Twenty-five Studies for Piano, Op. 47 Fifty Selected Studies (No. 2)
LE COUPPEY, F. (1811-1887)	Rustic Dance	WR	Rediscovered Classics, Bk. I (Henderson)
LIADOV, A. (1855-1914)	Russian Folk Song	BH	From Ancient To Modern (Rowley)
PLEYEL, I. (1757-1831)	Minuet and Trio in C	WR	Rediscovered Classics, Bk. I (Henderson)
SCHUMANN, R. (1810-1856)	Bagatelle, Op. 68, No. 5 (Little Piece)	P GS K Co GS	Album for the Young, Op. 68 Master Series for the Young
	Choral, Op. 68, No. 4	P GS K Co GS GS	Album for the Young, Op. 68 Selected Piano Solos by Romantic Composers, Bk. I Published separately
	Ditty, Op. 68, No. 3 (Humming Song)	P GS K Co GS GS GS	Album for the Young, Op. 68 Selected Piano Solos by Romantic Composers, Bk. I Master Series for the Young Published separately
	Melody, Op. 68, No. 1	P GS K Co GS PP GS A GS Su	Album for the Young, Op. 68 Master Series for the Young Hundred Best Short Classics, Bk. I Selected Piano Solos by Romantic Composers, Bk. I Beringer's School of Easy Classics: Schumann Published separately Piano Literature of the 17th, 18th and 19th Centuries, Bk. 4b (Clark)
	Soldier's March, Op. 68 No. 2	P GS	Album for the Young, Op. 68

Composer	Title	Publisher	Volume or Collection
SCHUMANN, R. (cont.)		K	
		Co	
		GS	Master Series for the Young
		PP	Hundred Best Short Classics, Bk. I
		He	A Little Treasury of Classics, Bk. II (Lambert)
		P	Sonatinen Vorstufe, Vol. I
		He	A Treasury of Easy Classics (Abrams)
		Su	Piano Literature of the 17th, 18th and 19th Centuries, Bk. 2 (Clark)
		GS	Published separately
	The Merry Farmer's Return from Work, Op. 68, No. 10 (The Merry Peasant)	P	Album for the Young, Op. 68
		GS	
		K	
		Co	
		GS	Master Series for the Young
		PP	Hundred Best Short Classics, Bk. I
		A	Beringer's School of Easy Classics: Schumann
		Su	Piano Literature of the 17th, 18th and 19th Centuries, Bk. 3 (Clark)
		P	Sonatinen Album, Vol. II
		GS	Published separately
		P	Sonatinen Vorstufe, Vol. I
		He	A Treasury of Easy Classics (Abrams)
TSCHAIKOWSKY, P. (1840-1893)	Old French Song, Op. 39, No. 16	GS	Master Series for the Young
		Su	Piano Literature of the 17th, 18th and 19th Centuries, Bk. 4b (Clark)
	The Doll's Burial, Op. 39, No. 7	GS	Album for the Young, Op. 39
		P	
		Su	Piano Literature of the 17th, 18th and 19th Centuries, Bk. 3 (Clark)
	The Sick Doll, Op. 39, No. 6	GS	Album for the Young, Op. 39
		P	
WEBER, C. (1786-1826)	Ecossaise in F	He	A Little Treasury of Classics, Bk. I (Lambert)
	Ecossaise in G		

Composer	Title	Publisher	Volume or Collection
BADINGS, HENK (1907-)	From "Arcadia," Bk. 3, Nos. 1-4; 6, 8, 10	Sch	Arcadia, Bk. 3
	Burlesque, From "Arcadia"	Su	Musical Finds from the 20th Century (Podolsky)
	Scale Tune		
	Ten Pieces	Sch	Arcadia, Bk. 2
BARTÓK, BÉLA (1881-1945)	A Little Dance (No. 5 from First Term at the Piano)	Su	Musical Finds from the 20th Century (Podolsky)
	Ballade (No. 13 from "For Children, Vol. I")	Su	Contemporary Piano Literature, Bk. 5 (Clark)
	Children At Play (No. 1 from "For Children, Vol. I")	Su	Contemporary Piano Literature, Bk. 2 (Clark)
		BH	From Ancient to Modern (Rowley)
	Children's Game (No. 12 from "For Children, Vol. I")	Su	Contemporary Piano Literature, Bk. 4 (Clark)
	Children's Game (No. 15 from "For Children, Vol. I")	Su	Contemporary Piano Literature, Bk. 3 (Clark)
	Dance of the Slovaks	K	Ten Easy Pieces For Children
	Eighteen Elementary Pieces	K BH	The First Term At The Piano
	Folk Dance (No. 1 from First Term at the Piano)	Su	Musical Finds from the 20th Century (Podolsky)
	Folksong	K BH	Ten Easy Pieces For Children
	(Poco Andante)	I Sch	Sixteen Pieces for Children (No. 3) The New Piano Book, II
	From "For Children," Vol. I, Nos. 1-11; 13-20; 22, 24, 25, 27, 29, 30, 31, 34	BH	For Children, Vol. I
	From "For Children," Vol. II, Nos. 1-10; 12-17; 19, 20, 23, 24, 28, 30, 31, 32, 35, 38	BH	For Children, Vol. II

Composer	Title	Publisher	Volume or Collection
BARTÓK, BÉLA (cont.)	From "Hungarian Folk Melodies", Nos. 1-11; 13-20; 22, 24, 25, 27, 29, 32, 33, 36	L	42 Hungarian Folk Melodies (Same contents as "For Children," Vol. I except Nos. 25 and 31)
	From "Sixteen Pieces for Children", Nos. 1-8; 12-15	I	16 Pieces for Children (Contents selected from "For Children, Vol. I" and "Ten Easy Pieces for Children")
	In Yugoslav Mode	BH	Mikrokosmos, Vol. II
	Jeering Song	BH	For Children, Vol. I (No. 30)
		Su	Contemporary Piano Literature, Bk. 4 (Clark)
	(Allegro ironico)	Sch	The New Piano Book, Bk. I
		L	42 Hungarian Folk Melodies
	Jest	BH	For Children, Vol. I (No. 27)
		Su	Contemporary Piano Literature, Bk. 5 (Clark)
	Meditation	BH	Mikrokosmos, Vol. II
	Minuetto		
	My Doll Is Lost	BH	For Children, Vol. I (No. 3)
		Su	Musical Finds from the 20th Century (Podolsky)
	Not Too Fast	MMC	Meet Modern Music, Part I
	Peasant's Dance	K	The First Term at the Piano (No. 17) Contemporary Piano Literature, Bk. 3 (Clark)
	Peasant's Song	K	Ten Easy Pieces for Children
		I	16 Pieces for Children
		MMC	Meet Modern Music, Part I
	Play	BH	For Children, Vol. I (No. 5)
		Su	Contemporary Piano Literature, Bk. 3 (Clark)
	Play Song	BH	For Children, Vol. I (No. 7)
		Su	Contemporary Piano Literature, Bk. 3 (Clark)
	Soldier's Song (No. 18 from "For Children, Vol. I")	Su	Contemporary Piano Literature, Bk. 4 (Clark)
	Song of the Wanderer (No. 7 from "For Children, Vol. II")	Su	Musical Finds from the 20th Century (Podolsky)
	The Bagpipe	Sch	The New Piano Book, Vol. I
	Two Folk Songs (Nos. 1 and 10 from "First Term at the Piano")	Su	Contemporary Piano Literature, Bk. 2 (Clark)
	Two Peasant Dances (No. 16 from "First Term at	Su	Contemporary Piano Literature, Bk. 4 (Clark)

Composer	Title	Publisher	Volume or Collection
BARTÓK, BÉLA (cont.)	the Piano" and No. 14 from "For Children, Vol. I")		
	Where Have You Been, My Lambkin (No. 15 from "First Term at the Piano")	Su	Contemporary Piano Literature, Bk. 3 (Clark)
BLANCHET, E. (1877-1943)	"L'Album de Nanette" 1st Series 1. Premier Pas 2. Cloches Joyeuses 3. Petite Romance 2nd Series 1. Monsieur Polichinelle 2. Il Etait une Bergére 3. Nous n'irons plus au-bois	E	L'Album de Nanette
BOWLES, PAUL (1910-)	"Folk Preludes" 1. Peter Gray 2. Ching A Ring Chaw 4. Oh! Potatoes They Grow Small Over There	MMC	Folk Preludes
COWELL, HENRY (1897-)	Sway Dance	MMI	Published Separately
DIAMOND, DAVID (1915-)	Eight Piano Pieces 1. Pease-Porridge Hot 2. Jumping Jacks 3. The Old Mr. Turtle 4. Handy-Spandy, Jack-A-Dandy 5. Jack and Jill 6. Rock-A-Bye, Baby 7. Little Jumping Joan 8. Lullaby	GS	Eight Piano Pieces
DROSDOFF, A. (1889-1950)	Ukranian Song	W	Modern Russian Piano Music By Contemporary Composers
FINNEY, ROSS LEE (1906-)	From "Inventions"	Su	Inventions
	1. There and Back	Su	Contemporary Piano Literature, Bk. 4 (Clark)
	2. Berceuse	Su	Contemporary Piano Literature, Bk. 4 (Clark)
	3. Puzzle 4. Barcarolle 5. Skipping	Su	Contemporary Piano Literature, Bk. 4 (Clark)
	6. Searching 7. Tired		

Composer	Title	Publisher	Volume or Collection
FREED, ISADORE (1900-1960)	Around the Maypole	CF	Published Separately
	Punchinello		
	Story at Evening		
GOEDICKE, ALEXANDER (1877-)	Hopak	L	The Student Pianist, Vol. I (Mirovitch)
	Sadness		
	In India		
	The Blacksmith Works		
	Marlborough Goes to Work		
GREEN, RAY (1909-)	March Sonatina, No. 1	AME	Published separately
	Polka Sonatina, No. 1		
	Summer Smoke		

GRETCHANINOFF,
ALEXANDER
(1864-1956)
	Album d'Andrucha, Op. 133
	  1. Old Children's Song
	  2. Little Dreamer
	  3. Naughty Girl
	  4. Little Elegant
	  5. The Dance of the
	     Goldfishes
	  6. The Mountebank
	  7. Gallant Cavalier
	  8. My Little Dog Joujou
	  9. Invitation to a Walk
	 10. Children's Dance
		E	Album d'Andrucha, Op. 133

	Children's Book, Op. 98
	  1. Fairy Tale
	  2. The Tin Soldiers in
	     Camp
	  3. The Tin Soldiers
	     Marching
	  4. Farewell
	  5. Riding the Hobby-
	     Horse
	  6. In the Woodland Glade
	  7. Njanja Being Ill
	  8. A Tiresome Lesson
	  9. Cradle Song
	 10. A Little Dance
	 11. A Terrible Event
	 12. A Study
	 13. After the Ball
	 14. The Little Traveller
	 15. The Little Would-Be
	     Man
		Sch
		I
			Children's Book, Op. 98

	Complaint, Op. 123	Su	Contemporary Piano Literature, Bk. 4 (Clark)

Composer	Title	Publisher	Volume or Collection

GRETCHANINOFF, ALEXANDER (cont.)	Four Pieces From "Album de Nina," Op. 141
	  1. Reve d'Enfant
	  3. Aprés La Messe
	  7. Au Rouet
	  9. Nuages Du Soir
		E	Album de Nina, Op. 141

	Four Pieces from "A Child's Day," Op. 109
	  1. Morning Prayer
	  2. At Work
	  3. My Little Horse
	  4. The Broken Toy
		Sch M	A Child's Day, Op. 109

	Glass Beads, Op. 123	K L	Glass Beads, Op. 123
	1. Morning Walk	Su	Contemporary Piano Literature, Bk. 3 (Clark)
	2. Little Beggar	Su	Contemporary Piano Literature, Bk. 3 (Clark)
	3. Etude		
	4. Sad Song		
	5. On The Bicycle (Bicycle ride)	Su	Contemporary Piano Literature, Bk. 4 (Clark)
	6. Waltz	Su	Contemporary Piano Literature, Bk. 4
	7. Heavy Work		
	8. My First Ball	Su	Contemporary Piano Literature, Bk. 3
	9. Complaint	Su	Contemporary Piano Literature, Bk. 4
	10. In the Fields		
	11. Mother's Caress		
	12. On the Harmonica		

	Twelve Little Sketches, Op. 182
	  1. Sunrise
	  2. With the Fishing Rod
	  3. Returning Home with a Bouquet of Flowers
	  4. The Orphan
	  5. A New Friend
	  6. On the Swing
	  7. At Grandmother's
	  8. Country Lad
	  9. Asking for a New Doll
	10. The New Doll
	11. Tag
	12. It's Time to Go Home
		I	Twelve Little Sketches For Children, Op. 182

	Waltz, Op. 123	Su	Contemporary Piano Literature, Bk. 4 (Clark)
JACOBI, FREDERICK (1891-1952)	Once Upon A Time	CF	Published Separately

Composer	Title	Publisher	Volume or Collection
KABALEVSKY, DMITRI (1904-)	A Game, Op. 39	Su	Contemporary Piano Literature, Bk. 1 (Clark)
	A Gay Little Story (No. 14, "Fairy Tale")	Su I	Contemporary Piano Literature, Bk. 2 24 Little Pieces for Children, Op. 39
	A Little Joke	Su	Contemporary Piano Literature, Bk. 2 (Clark)
	(No. 12, "Joke", Op. 39)	I	24 Little Pieces for Children, Op. 39
	A Little Song	L I Su	15 Pieces for Children, Op. 27, Bk. I 18 Pieces for Children, Op. 27 Contemporary Piano Literature, Bk. 3 (Clark)
	A Merry Tale, Op. 39	Su	Musical Finds from the 20th Century (Podolsky)
	Country Dance, Op. 34, No. 17	L	The Student Pianist, Vol. I (Mirovitch)
	Dancing, Op. 39	Su	Musical Finds from the 20th Century (Podolsky)
	(Dance)	Su	Contemporary Piano Literature, Bk. 1 (Clark)
	Galloping, Op. 39 (Hurdling)	Su	Contemporary Piano Literature, Bk. 2 (Clark)
	Hopping, Op. 39, No. 18 (Gallop)	Su	Contemporary Piano Literature, Bk. 3 (Clark)
	Little Pieces for Children, Op. 39, Nos. 1-20	I	24 Little Pieces for Children, Op. 39
	Moonlight on the River	I	18 Pieces for Children, Op. 27
	Playing Ball	L I	15 Pieces for Children, Op. 27, Bk. I 18 Pieces for Children, Op. 27
	Polka, Op. 39	Su	Contemporary Piano Literature, Bk. 1 (Clark)
	Quick March	Su	Contemporary Piano Literature, Bk. 5 (Clark)
	(Marionettes, No. 10)	I	24 Little Pieces for Children, Op. 39
	Running Along, Op. 39, No. 6	Su	Contemporary Piano Literature, Bk. 1 (Clark)
		L	The Student Pianist, Vol. I (Mirovitch)
	(Scherzino)	I	24 Little Pieces for Children, Op. 39
	Selected Piano Pieces for Children Nos. 1, 2, 3, 4, 6, 7	P	Kabalevsky, Selected Piano Pieces for Children
	Singing, Op. 39, No. 8	L	The Student Pianist, Vol. I (Mirovitch)
	The Clown, Op. 39	Su	Musical Finds from the 20th Century (Podolsky)
		Su	Contemporary Piano Literature, Bk. 3 (Clark)

Composer	Title	Publisher	Volume or Collection
KABALEVSKY, DMITRI (cont.)	The Little Twins, Op. 39, No. 7	L	The Student Pianist, Vol. I (Mirovitch)
KODÁLY, ZOLTÁN (1882-)	Children's Dances 1. Allegretto 2. Allegretto Cantabile 3. Vivace	BH	Children's Dances
MAYKAPAR, SAMUEL (1867-1938)	From "18 Selected Pieces" 1. In the Garden, Op. 28 2. Waltz, Op. 33 4. Dew drops 5. The Little Music Box, Op. 28 6. The Little Shepherd, Op. 28 7. Passing Fancy, Op. 28 8. The Moth, Op. 28 9. Autumn, Op. 28 11. Echo in the Mountains, Op. 28 16. Little Story, Op. 28 17. Little Fairy Tale, Op. 8	L L L L L L	18 Selected Pieces; Maykapar (Mirovitch) The Student Pianist (Mirovitch) The Student Pianist (Mirovitch) The Student Pianist (Mirovitch) The Student Pianist (Mirovitch) The Student Pianist (Mirovitch)
MIASKOWSKY, NICOLAI (1881-1951)	Carefree	W	Modern Russian Piano Music
MILHAUD, DARIUS (1892-)	Touches Blanches Touches Noires	CF	Masters of Our Day; 18 Solos in the Contemporary Idiom
MOORE, DOUGLAS (1893-)	Decoration Day Mississippi Careful Etta Fiddlin' Joe Grievin' Annie	Su CF	Contemporary Piano Literature, Bk. 3 (Clark) Masters of Our Day; 18 Solos in the Contemporary Idiom
PAZ, JUAN (1897-)	Pampeana	CF	Published Separately
PERSICHETTI, V. (1915-)	Parades, Op. 57 1. March 2. Canter 3. Pomp Selections from Op. 60 1. Berceuse	EV EV	Parades for Piano, Op. 57 Little Piano Book, Op. 60

Composer	Title	Publisher	Volume or Collection
PERSICHETTI, V. (cont.)	2. Capriccio		
	3. Dialogue		
	4. Masque		
	5. Statement		
	6. Arietta		
	10. Prologue		
	11. Canon		
	12. Epilogue		
PHILLIPS, BURRILL (1907-)	Little Song	EV	Published Separately
PONCE, MANUEL (1882-1948)	Easy Pieces, Based on Mexican Folk Tunes	So	20 Piezas Faciles Para Piano
	3. Los Xtoles		
	4. Danza De La Lluvia		
	5. Cancion De La Lluvia		
	6. Danza De Los Tecuanes		
	7. Cancion Campesina		
	9. Las Mañanitas		
	11. La Pasadita		
	12. La Sandunga		
	13. Ven¡ Oh Luna!		
	16. La Posada		
	17. La Revolucion		
	18. La Cucaracha		
	20. La Patria		
REBIKOV, VLADIMIR (1866-1920)	Accompanimento ostinato	Sch	Piano Album, No. II (Rowley)
	A Little Girl Pleading with her Mother (Une Fillette Implore Sa Mère)	I Sch	Pictures for Children, Op. 37 Piano Album No. II (Rowley)
	Languorous Dance		
	Persuasion		
	The Bear		
REVUELTAS, SILVESTRE (1899-1940)	Canción	CF	Published Separately
RHENE-BATON (1879-1940)	Une petite chanson (A Little Song)	E E MMC	Pour Yvonne Published Separately Meet Modern Music, Part I
	Une petite gavotte	E E	Pour Yvonne Published Separately
	Une petite valse	E E MMC	Pour Yvonne Published Separately Meet Modern Music, Part I

Composer	Title	Publisher	Volume or Collection
ROBB, J. D. (1892-)	Pictures of New Mexico In the Cottonwood Grove In the Indian Village Siesta Time The Bells of the Mission	AMP	Published Separately
RUBINSTEIN, BERYL (1898-1953)	Tally-Ho Wildflowers Butterflies	CF	A Day in the Country

	Musical Fancies, Series I
	  1. The Cuckoo
	  2. Valse
	  3. Gavotte
	  4. Song without Words
	  5. Puck
		CF	Published Separately

SAMINSKY, LAZARE (1882-)	Old Veranda, Op. 45, No. 1 from "Cynthia's Play-nook"	CF	Masters of Our Day
SATIE, ERIK (1866-1925)	Petit prélude à la journée Berceuse Marche du grand escalier	E	Enfantillages pittoresques

	Menus propos Enfantine
	  1. Chant guerrier du roi des hericots (War Song of the Bean King)
	  2. Ce que Dit la Petite Princesse des Tulips (The Tulip Princess Says)
	    Valse du Chocolat aux Amandes (Waltz of the Chocolate Bar)
		E
		MMC
			Menus propos Enfantines
			Meet Modern Music, Part I

SCOTT, CYRIL (1879-)	See Saw (From "My Young Friends")	Su	Contemporary Piano Literature, Bk. 3 (Clark)
SHOSTAKOVITCH, DMITRI (1906-)	Children's Pieces	L	Six Children's Pieces
	1. March	Su	Contemporary Piano Literature, Bk. 2 (Clark)
	2. Waltz	Su	Contemporary Piano Literature, Bk. 2 (Clark)
	3. The Bear	Co	The Solo Book, Vol. III (Zeetlin and Goldberger)
	4. A Happy Fairy Tale	L Su	Published Separately Contemporary Piano Literature, Bk. 3 (Clark)
	(Gay Story)	Su	Musical Finds from the 20th Century (Podolsky)

Composer	Title	Publisher	Volume or Collection
SHOSTAKOVITCH, DMITRI	(Gay Story)	BH	From Ancient to Modern (Rowley)
	5. A Sad Fairy Tale	Su	Contemporary Piano Literature, Bk. 3 (Clark)
	6. The Mechanical Doll	Su	Contemporary Piano Literature, Bk. 3 (Clark)
		L	Published Separately
SIEGMEISTER, ELIE (1909-)	Song of the Dark Street Games	Su	Contemporary Piano Literature, Bk. 2 (Clark)
	Three Pieces Lazy Sam Lullaby Havin' Fun	Su	Contemporary Piano Literature, Bk. 1 (Clark)
STRAVINSKY, IGOR (1882-)	Andantino (Just Walking)	O MMC	The Five Fingers Meet Modern Music, Part I
TANSMAN, ALEXANDRE (1897-)	Melody	L L	Children at Play Published Separately
	From "Pour les Enfants," First Set 5. Valse des mario- nettes 7. Dresden China Figures 8. Vacation is over 10. The Firemen 12. Conclusion	E	Pour les Enfants, First Set
	From "Pour les Enfants," Second Set 1. Stroll 2. In the Garden 3. Mazurka 4. The Arithmetic Lesson 6. Solemn Occasion	E	Pour les Enfants, Second Set
	Three Pieces A Little Song Bouncing Ball Folk Dance	Su	Contemporary Piano Literature, Bk. 1 (Clark)
	Chromatics	Su	Contemporary Piano Literature, Bk. 2 (Clark)
	Peasant Tune		
TCHÉREPNINE, ALEXANDRE (1899-)	Three Pieces March Joy and Tears Relays	Su	Contemporary Piano Literature, Bk. 1 (Clark)

Composer	Title	Publisher	Volume or Collection
TCHÉREPNINE, ALEXANDRE (cont.)	Three Pieces Chimes Melody To and Fro	Su	Contemporary Piano Literature, Bk. 2 (Clark)
	Old Tale	Su	Contemporary Piano Literature, Bk. 4 (Clark)
	Three Pieces Hide and Seek The Clock Prelude	Su	Contemporary Piano Literature, Bk. 3 (Clark)
VILLA-LOBOS, HEITOR (1887-1960)	From "The Toy Wheel" 1. Put Your Little Foot Out 2. The Carranquinha Mode 5. Garabaldi Went To Mass 6. Let Us All Go To Dance	PI	Published Separately

SECTION II

UPPER ELEMENTARY

GRADES III AND IV

MUSIC OF THE SIXTEENTH, SEVENTEENTH
AND EIGHTEENTH CENTURIES

Composer	Title	Publisher	Volume or Collection
ARNE, T. A. (1710-1778)	Country Dance	BMC	Purcell-Arne Album
	Figure Dance		
	Jig		
	March from "Alfred"		
	Minuet in G		
	Sailor's Dance		
	Siciliano		
BACH, C. P. E. (1714-1788)	Allegro in A Minor	K	The Direct Path (Hermann)
	Allegro in C Minor	C	Eighteenth Century Music, Vol. I
	Allegro in D	H	The Sons of Bach
		Su	Piano Literature of the 17th, 18th and 19th Centuries, Bk. 5a (Clark)
	Allegro in D	C	Eighteenth Century Music, Vol. II
	Allegro in E-flat	H	The Sons of Bach
	Allegro in G	H	The Sons of Bach
	Andante	U	Old Masters For Young Pianists, Bk. 1 (Kuranda)
	La Caroline	H	The Sons of Bach
		Su	Piano Literature of the 17th, 18th and 19th Centuries, Bk. 4a (Clark)
	La Xenophone	SG	Classics from the Seventeenth and Eighteenth Centuries (Tapper)
		U	Clavierstücke, C. P. E. Bach
	Little Fantasy in D Minor	U	Old Masters for Young Pianists, Bk. 1 (Kuranda)
	Minuet in A	BH	From Ancient To Modern (Rowley)
		Su	Piano Literature of the 17th, 18th and 19th Centuries, Bk. 5a (Clark)
	Minuet in C	U	Clavierstücke, C. P. E. Bach
	Minuet in G	C	Eighteenth Century Music, Vol. II (No. 3)
	Solfeggietto	He	A Treasury of Easy Classics (Abrams)
		B	Hours with the Masters, Bk. V
		CF	Road to Piano Artistry, Vol. VI (Scionti)
		Sch	Die Söhne Bach
		GS	Published Separately
		Su	Piano Literature of the 17th, 18th and 19th Centuries, Bk. 5a (Clark)

31

Composer	Title	Publisher	Volume or Collection
BACH, C. P. E. (cont.)	Two Alternate Minuets	U	Clavierstücke, C. P. E. Bach
	Two Minuets in A		
BACH, J. C. F. (1732-1795)	Angloise	Sch	Clavierstücke für Anfänger
	Minuet to Dance in D	Sch	Menuetten fürs Clavier
		H	The Sons of Bach
	Schwaebisch in F	Sch	Clavierstücke für Anfänger
BACH, J. S. (1685-1750)	Applicatio	K	Bach's Little Notebook for Wilhelm Friedmann Bach
	Aria, "Gedenke doch mein Geist" (Pray, Remember My Soul)	K	Little Notebook for Anna Magdalena Bach (pg. 119)
		GS	Master Series for the Young (pg. 5)
	Bourrée in A	K	The First Bach Book
	Bourrée in B Minor	B	Hours with the Masters, Bk. III
	Bourrée in E Minor	GS	First Lessons in Bach, Bk. I (Carroll)
		BH	Airs and Dances, Bk. 2 (Dorolle)
		P	Sonatinen Album, Vol. II
		CF	Bach First Lessons, Bk. I (Carroll)
		GS	Master Series for the Young
		K	The First Bach Book
		CF	Road to Piano Artistry, Vol. II (Scionti)
	Chorale, "Schaff's mit mir, Gott" (Do As Thou Wills't with Me O Lord)	K	Little Notebook of Anna Magdalena Bach
	Gavotte in G Minor	GS	First Lessons in Bach, Bk. I (Carroll)
		CF	Bach First Lessons, Bk. I (Carroll)
		PP	Hundred Best Short Classics, Bk. I
		B	Hours with the Masters, Bk. III
	Little Prelude in C	BMC	Bach for Early Grades, Bk. II (pg. 18)
		GS	Eighteen Little Preludes and Fugues (No. 15)
		Sch	Little Piano Book of Wilhelm Friedemann Bach (No. 2)
		GS	Master Series for the Young (pg. 19)
		GS	Short Preludes and Fugues (No. 1)
		K	The First Bach Book (No. 18)
		K	Short Preludes and Fugues (No. 1)
		P	Short Preludes and Fugues (pg. 2)
		P	Sonatinen Album, Vol. II
		Su	Piano Literature of the 17th, 18th and 19th Centuries, Bk. 5a (Clark)
	Little Prelude in C	GS	Eighteen Little Preludes and Fugues (No. 9)
		K	First Bach Book (No. 19)
		Sch	Little Piano Book of Wilhelm Friedemann Bach
		GS	Master Series for the Young (pg. 14)

Composer	Title	Publisher	Volume or Collection
BACH, J. S. (cont.)		U	Old Masters for Young Pianists (Kuranda) (Bk. I)
		GS	Short Preludes and Fugues (No. 2)
		K	Short Preludes and Fugues (No. 2)
		P	Short Preludes and Fugues (No. 2)
		Su	Piano Literature of the 17th, 18th and 19th Centuries, Bk. 5a (Clark)
		ECS	Bach Verklärt (Not. 25)
	Little Prelude in C Minor	GS	Eighteen Little Preludes and Fugues (No. 4)
		K	First Bach Book (No. 21)
		GS	Master Series for the Young (pg. 15)
		CF	Road to Piano Artistry, Vol. II (pg. 8)
		GS	Short Preludes and Fugues (No. 3)
		K	Short Preludes and Fugues (No. 3)
		P	Short Preludes and Fugues (No. 3)
	March in D	CF	Bach First Lessons, Bk. I (Carroll)
		BMC	Bach for Early Grades, Bk. I
		GS	First Lessons in Bach, Bk. I (Carroll)
		PP	Hundred Best Short Classics, Bk. I
		K	Little Notebook for Anna Magdalena Bach, (pg. 60)
		GS	Master Series for the Young
		P	Notenbuch der Anna Magdalena Bach (Sauer)
		K	The First Bach Book
		Su	Piano Literature of the 17th, 18th and 19th Centuries, Bk. 3 (Clark)
		K	Bach and His Contemporaries
		WR	Rediscovered Classics, Bk. 1 (Henderson)
	March in E-flat	BMC	Bach for Early Grades, Bk. II (In C Major)
		K	Little Notebook for Anna Magdalena Bach
		GS	Master Series for the Young
		P	Notenbuch der Anna Magdalena Bach (Sauer)
		K	The First Bach Book
	March in G	CF	Bach First Lessons, Bk. I (Carroll)
		BMC	Bach for Early Grades, Bk. I
		GS	First Lessons in Bach, Bk. I (Carroll)
		K	Little Notebook for Anna Magdalena Bach
		P	Notenbuch der Anna Magdalena Bach (Sauer)
		K	The First Bach Book
	Menuet in A Minor	K	Little Notebook for Anna Magdalena Bach (pg. 58)
		P	Notenbuch der Anna Magdalena Bach (Sauer)
		I	The Little Music Book for Anna Magdalena Bach
	Menuet in B-flat	K	The Little Notebook for Anna Magdalena Bach (pg. 53)
		K	The First Bach Book

Composer	Title	Publisher	Volume or Collection
BACH, J. S. (cont.)	Menuet in C Minor	BMC	Bach for Early Grades, Bk. I
		CF	Bach First Lessons, Bk. I (Carroll)
		GS	First Lessons in Bach, Bk. I (Carroll)
		K	The Little Notebook for Anna Magdalena Bach
		K	The First Bach Book
		Su	Piano Literature of the 17th, 18th and 19th Centuries, Bk. 3 (Clark)
	Menuet in E	CF	Bach First Lessons, Bk. II (Carroll)
		GS	First Lessons in Bach, Bk. II (Carroll)
		K	French Suites, No. 6 in E
		P	French Suites
		GS	French Suites
		GS	Master Series for the Young
		U	Old Masters for Young Pianists (Kuranda) Bk. I
		ECS	Bach Verklärt
	Menuet in F	K	Little Notebook for Anna Magdalena Bach (pg. 42)
		P	Notenbuch der Anna Magdalena Bach (Sauer)
		K	The First Bach Book
		I	The Little Music Book for Anna Magdalena Bach
	Menuet in F	CF	Bach First Lessons, Bk. II (Carroll)
		GS	First Lessons in Bach, Bk. II (Carroll)
	Menuet in G	BMC	Bach for Early Grades, Bk. II
	Menuet in G (I)	Sch	Little Piano Book for Wilhelm Friedemann Bach
		CF	Road to Piano Artistry, Vol. III (Scionti)
	Menuet in G (III)	Sch	Little Piano Book for Wilhelm Friedemann Bach
	Menuet in G Minor (II)	BMC	Bach for Early Grades, Bk. II
		Sch	Little Piano Book for Wilhelm Friedemann Bach
		K	The First Bach Book (pg. 12)
	Menuet in G Minor	Sch	Little Piano Book for Wilhelm Friedemann Bach (pg. 9)
	Polonaise in D Minor	BMC	Bach for Early Grades, Bk. II
		K	Little Notebook for Anna Magdalena Bach (pg. 74)
		P	Notenbuch der Anna Magdalena Bach (pg. 15) (Sauer)
	Polonaise in G	CF	Bach First Lessons, Bk. II (Carroll)
		GS	First Lessons in Bach, Bk. II (Carroll)
		K	Little Notebook for Anna Magdalena Bach (pg. 82)
		P	Notenbuch der Anna Magdalena Bach (pg. 18) (Sauer)

Composer	Title	Publisher	Volume or Collection
BACH, J. S. (cont.)	Prelude in C	BMC	Bach for Early Grades, Bk. III (pg. 4)
		K	Little Notebook for Anna Magdalena Bach (pg. 84)
		GS	Master Series for the Young (pg. 22)
		PP	Hundred Best Short Classics, Bk. II
		K	Well Tempered Clavier, Bk. I (No. 1)
		ECS	Bach Verklärt
		K	Bach's Little Notebook for Wilhelm Friedmann Bach (No. 14)
		P	Sonatinen Album, Vol. I
	Prelude in E Minor	BMC	Bach for Early Grades, Bk. II
BACH, W. F. (1710-1784)	Minuet in G	CF	Road to Piano Artistry, Vol. I (Scionti)
BARRETT, J. (1674-1735 or 1736)	Rigaudon (The St. Catherine	H	Contemporaries of Purcell
		BH	Old English Worthies
		GS	Early Classics for the Piano (Mirovitch)
BENDA, F. (1709-1786)	Minuet in G	Sch	Menuetten fürs Clavier
BLOW, J. (1649-1708)	Theatre Tune	H	Contemporaries of Purcell
BYRD, W. (1542-1623)	Rowland	BH	Airs and Dances, Bk. I (Dorolle)
CLARKE, J. (1670-1707)	Ayre in C	H	Contemporaries of Purcell
CLÉRAMBAULT, L. (1676-1749)	Allegro in D Minor	BH	Airs and Dances, Bk. I (Dorolle)
CORELLI, A. (1653-1713)	Gavotte	K	Easy Pieces From Old Italian Masters
	Sarabande in E Minor	P	Sonatinen Vorstufe, Vol. II
		K	Easy Pieces From Old Italian Masters
		K	Corelli, 24 Pieces for the Piano, Vol. 1
		BH	Sonatinen Vorstufe, Vol. II
COUPERIN, F. (1668-1733)	Bourdon	BH	Airs and Dances, Bk. I (Dorolle)
	Fanfare in D	U	Old Masters for Young Pianists, Bk. I (Kuranda)
		U	Grosse Meister für Kleine Hande, Bk. 1, (Kuranda)
	Les Coucous	BH	Airs and Dances, Bk. II (Dorolle)
	Le Dodo	BH	Airs and Dances, Bk. I (Dorolle)
	L'Epineuse	BH	Airs and Dances, Bk. I (Dorolle)
	Le Petit Rien	PP	Hundred Best Short Classics, Bk. I
		SG	Classics from the Seventeenth and Eighteenth Centuries (Tapper)
		He	A Treasury of Easy Classics (Abrams)

Composer	Title	Publisher	Volume or Collection
COUPERIN, F. (cont.)	Passepied in D	BH	Airs and Dances, Bk. I (Dorolle)
	The Knitters	U	Old Masters for Young Pianists, Bk. I (Kuranda)
		U	Grosse Meister für Kleine Hände, Bk. I (Kuranda)
DANDRIEU, de (1684-1740)	The Fifers	BH SG	Airs and Dances, Bk. I (Dorolle) Classics from the Seventeenth and Eighteenth Centuries (Tapper)
DAQUIN, C. (1694-1772)	Tambourin	He	A Little Treasury of Classics, Bk. II (Lambert)
DIABELLI, A. (1781-1858)	Andante in B-flat (From Sonatina in F)	WR	Rediscovered Classics, Bk. I (Henderson)
DUSSEK, J. (1760-1812)	Minuetto in G	B	Hours with the Masters, Bk. III
	Menuett with Variation	P	Sonatinen Vorstufe, Vol. I
FARNABY, G. (1565-1600)	A Toye	He	A Little Treasury of Classics, Bk. II (Lambert)
FISCHER, J. K. F. (1650-1746)	Bourrée in A Minor	GS	Introduction to Piano Classics, Vol. I (Mirovitch)
	Fugue in C	K	A Little Book of Fugues

	From "The Notebook"
	  Bourrée in F
	  Marche de Landau
	  Menuet in A Minor
	  Menuet in A Minor
	  Menuet in C
	  Menuet in F
	  Menuet in G
	  Sarabande in A Minor
		Sch	The Notebook of Johann Kaspar Ferd. Fischer
			
			(No. 15)
			(No. 9)
			
			(No. 11)
			(No. 13)

GLÄSER, C. L. T. (1747-1797)	Angloise in F	Sch	Clavierstücke für Anfänger
	Minuetto in B-flat		
	Minuetto in F		
GRAUPNER, C. (1683-1760)	Air (From Suite in G)	P	Contemporaries of Telemann
	Air en Gavotte in C		
	Gavotte in G		
	Menuett in D		
	Menuett (From Suite in F)		
GROSSE, M. C. (2nd Half of 18th Century)	Minuetto I in G	Sch	Menuetten fürs Clavier
	Minuetto II in G Minor		

Composer	Title	Publisher	Volume or Collection
GRÜNWALD, G. (1673-1739)	Gavotte in C	P	Contemporaries of Telemann
	Menuett I and II in A Minor		
	Menuett (From Partita in G)		
	Sarabande in A Minor		
HANDEL, G. F. (1685-1759)	Air in B-flat	Sch	Aylesford Pieces (No. 13)
		Sch	Pieces for Harpsichord, Vol. II (No. 39)
	Bourrée in D Minor	Sch	Twenty Little Dances
	Bourrée in G		
	Bourrée in G Minor		
	Gavotte in G	He	A Little Treasury of Classics, Bk. II (Lambert)
		Sch	Twenty Little Dances (Rigaudon, No. 15)
	Impertinence	Sch	Aylesford Pieces (No. 6)
		Sch	Pieces for Harpsichord, Vol. II (No. 51)
	Marsch in D	Sch	Twenty Little Dances
	Menuet in A Minor	Sch	Pieces for Harpsichord, Vol. I (No. 8)
		Sch	Aylesford Pieces (No. 19)
	Menuet in B Minor	Sch	Pieces for Harpsichord, Vol. II (No. 71)
	Menuet in B-flat	Sch	Twenty Little Dances, (No. 14)
		Sch	Pieces for Harpsichord, Vol. II (No. 66)
	Menuet in D	Sch	Aylesford Pieces (No. 10)
		Sch	Pieces for Harpsichord, Vol. II (No. 57)
	Menuet in D	Sch	Aylesford Pieces (No. 12)
			Pieces for Harpsichord, Vol. II (No. 58)
	Menuet in D Minor	Sch	Aylesford Pieces (No. 9)
		Sch	Pieces for Harpsichord, Vol. II (No. 56)
	Menuet in F	Sch	Pieces for Harpsichord, Vol. II (No. 61)
	Menuet in G Minor		(No. 64)
	Menuet in G Minor	Sch	Pieces for Harpsichord, Vol. I (No. 3)
	Menuet in G Minor	Sch	Pieces for Harpsichord, Vol. I (No. 4)
	Menuet in G Minor	Sch	Twenty Little Dances (No. 19)
	Menuetto in F Minor (No. 1)	GS	Twelve Easy Pieces (No. 2)
	Menuetto in F (No. 2)		
	Minuet in A	Sch	Pieces for Harpsichord, Vol. II (No. 69)
	Minuet in A		(No. 70)
	Minuet in B-flat		(No. 72)
	Minuet in B-flat		(No. 73)

Composer	Title	Publisher	Volume or Collection
HANDEL, G. F. (cont.)	Minuet in B-flat		(No. 74)
	Minuet in B-flat		(No. 75)
	Minuet in F		(No. 62)
	Minuet in F	Sch	Pieces for Harpsichord, Vol. I (No. 14)
	Minuet in G		Pieces for Harpsichord, Vol. II (No. 63)
	Minuet in G		Pieces for Harpsichord, Vol. I (No. 28)
	Minuet in G Minor		(No. 11)
	Passepied in A	Sch	Aylesford Pieces (No. 18)
		Sch	Pieces for Harpsichord, Vol. I (No. 7)
	Passepied in C	Sch	Pieces for Harpsichord, Vol. II (No. 76)
	Sarabands I and II in D-minor	K	Bach and His Contemporaries
	Sonatina in B-flat	BH	Airs and Dances, Bk. 2 (Dorolle)
		H	Easiest Original Pieces
		GS	Handel, 12 Easy Pieces
		GS	Master Series for the Young
		Su	Piano Literature of the 17th, 18th and 19th Centuries, Bk. 5a (Clark)
HÄSSLER, J. (1747-1822)	Allegro in C	GS	Introduction to Piano Classics, Vol. II (Mirovitch)
		Sch	Simple Short Piano Pieces (14a and 14b)
	Minuetto I in C	Sch	Menuetten fürs Clavier
	Minuetto II in C Minor		
	Minuetto in C		
	Minuetto in F		
HAYDN, J. (1732-1809)	Allegretto	K	The Direct Path
	Allegretto risoluto in G	U	Little Dances for Young Folk (No. 2)
	Allegro con brio in D		(No. 3)
	Contredanse F	Su	Piano Literature of the 17th, 18th and 19th Centuries, Bk. 3 (Clark)
	Contradanse in C	Co	The Solo Book, Vol. III (Zeetlin and Goldberger)
	Allegro	K	Twelve Easy Pieces (No. 2)
		P	Sonatinas, Vol. I
		K	A First Haydn Book (pg. 4)
		GS	Early Classics for the Piano (Mirovitch)
	Allegro (Allegro in A)	K	Twelve Easy Pieces (No. 7)
		K	A First Hayden Book
	Andante con moto	K	Twelve Easy Pieces (No. 12)
		GS	Early Classics for the Piano (Mirovitch)
	Andante	K	Twelve Easy Pieces (No. 3)
		K	A First Hayden Book (pg. 5)

Composer	Title	Publisher	Volume or Collection
HAYDN, J. (cont.)	Andante grazioso	K	Twelve Easy Pieces (No. 1)
		K	A First Haydn Book
	Andantino, un poco allegretto	K	Twelve Easy Pieces (No. 8)
		K	A First Haydn Book
	Adagio cantabile (Minuet in B-flat)	K	Twelve Easy Pieces (No. 5)
		Su	Piano Literature of the 17th, 18th and 19th Centuries, Bk. 4a (Clark)
	Ländler in E-flat	WR	Rediscovered Classics, Bk. 3 (Henderson)
	La fete (Scherzo from Sonatina 4)	S	Le Petit Classique (Morhange-Motchane)
	Le carillon (Allegro from Sonatina 3)	S	Le Petit Classique
	Menuetten I and II in A-flat	P	Sonatas, Vol. IV (No. 41)
	Menuetto in A	P	Sonatas, Vol. II (No. 23)
	Menuetto in D	AMP	Six Sonatinas (No. 1)
	Menuet in G	AMP	Six Sonatinas (No. 6)
	Menuetto al Rovescio (from unpublished Sonata in A)	WR	Rediscovered Classics, Bk. 3
	Menuetto	K	Twelve Easy Pieces (No. 10)
		K	A First Haydn Book (pg. 8)
	Menuetto Giocoso in C	GS	Published Separately
		CF	Road to Piano Artistry, Vol. IV (Scionti)
	(Allegretto Giocoso) (Minuet in C)	U	Little Dances for Young Folk (No. 1)
		GS	Master Series for the Young
		He	A Treasury of Easy Classics (Abrams)
		Su	Piano Literature of the 17th, 18th and 19th Centuries, Bk. 5a (Clark)
	Minuet and Trio (from (State Library in Berlin)	WR	Rediscovered Classics, Bk. 4
	Minuet in B-flat	GS	Introduction to Piano Classics, Vol. I (Mirovitch)
	Minuet in D	P	Sonatas, Vol. II (No. 20)
		GS	Sonatas, Vol. II (No. 19)
		K	Sonatas, Vol. I (No. 19)
		U	Sonatas, Vol. II (No. 11)
		PP	Hundred Best Short Classics, Bk. 1
	Romanze in F	P	Sonatinen Vorstufe, Vol. 2
	Sonatina in C	AMP	Six Sonatinas (No. 2)
		P	Six Little Divertimenti, (No. 5)
		Su	Piano Literature of the 17th, 18th and 19th Centuries, Bk. 4a (Clark)
	Sonatina in G	AMP	Six Sonatinas (No. 3)
		P	Six Little Divertiments (No. 4)

Composer	Title	Publisher	Volume or Collection
HAYDN, J. (cont.)	Twelve Easy Pieces	K	Twelve Easy Pieces
	Vivace assai	K	Twelve Easy Pieces (No. 11)
		GS	Early Classics for the Piano (Mirovitch)
HILLER, J. (1728-1804)	Minuetto II in C	Sch	Simple Short Piano Pieces
	Minuet in F	GS	Introduction to Piano Classics, Vol. II (Mirovitch)
	Musette in C	Sch	Simple Short Piano Pieces (No. 1)
HOOK, J. (1746-1827)	Giocoso (From Sonatina in G)	He	Little Treasury of Sonatinas, Bk. I
	Sonatina in D Giocoso Menuet Country Dance	BH	Early English Sonatinas
	Sonatina in G Allegro non troppo Rondo pastorale		
KIRNBERGER, J. (1721-1783)	Bourée in A Minor	Su	Kirnberger Collection (Jonas)
	Fughetta in C	Sch	Clavierstücke für Anfänger
	Invention and Little Fugue	GS	Introduction to Piano Classics, Vol. I (Mirovitch)
	Menuet in B-flat	U	Grosse Meister für kleine Hände, Bk. 2
	Menuet in G-sharp	Su	Kirnberger Collection (Jonas)
	Menuet in E		
	Menuet in E-flat		
	Minuetto in A	Sch	Clavierstücke für Anfänger
		K	Bach and His Contemporaries
	Minuetto in C (Minuet in C)	Sch	Clavierstücke für Anfänger
		Su	Kirnberger Collection (Jonas)
	Minuet in C	GS	Introduction to Piano Classics, Vol. I
	Minuet in D	K	Bach and His Contemporaries
	Minuet in E		
	Polonaise in D	GS	Introduction to Piano Classics, Vol. I
	Polonaise in G Major	Su	Kirnberger Collection (Jonas)
	Rigaudon		
KREBS, J. (1713-1780)	Menuett in A Minor	p	Contemporaries of Telemann
	Minuetto in A	Sch	Menuetten fürs Clavier
KUHNAU, J. (1660-1722)	Aria in A	U	Grosse Meister für kleine Hände, Bk. 2 (Kuranda)
		U	Old Masters for Young Pianists, Bk. 2

Composer	Title	Publisher	Volume or Collection
KUHNAU, J. (cont.)	Gavotte in B Minor	GS	Introduction to Piano Classics, Vol. 1 (Mirovitch)
	Prelude from Partita V in G	U	Grosse Meister für kleine Hände, Bk. 2
		U	Old Masters for Young Pianists, Bk. 2 (Kuranda)
		GS	Introduction to Piano Classics, Vol. I (Mirovitch)
		K	Old Masters of the 16th, 17th and 18th Centuries
LÉVASSEUR, P. F. (1753 - ?)	Rondeau à l'Allemande	P	Sonatinen Vorstufe, Vol. I
LOEILLET, J. (1653-1728)	Cibel	H	Contemporaries of Purcell
	Minuet in E Minor		
MAICHELBECK, F. A. (1702-1750)	Buffone	U	Grosse Meister für kleine Hände, Bk. 2 (Kuranda)
		U	Old Masters for Young Pianists, Bk. 2
MOZART, L. (1719-1785)	Allegro in A	O	Piano Music for Young Wolfgang (No. 15)
	Allegro in C	Sch	Notebook for Nannerl Mozart (No. 20)
	Allegro in G		(No. 11)
		He	Nannerl Mozart's Piano Book (Kreutzer)
	Allegro Moderato	He	Nannerl Mozart's Piano Book
	Andante in B-flat	Sch	Notebook for Nannerl Mozart (No. 21)
	Aria in G Minor	O	Piano Music for Young Wolfgang (No. 19)
	Bourrée in C Minor	Sch	Notebook for Wolfgang
		O	Piano Music for Young Wolfgang (No. 13)
		GS	Early Classics for the Piano (Mirovitch)
	The Hunt	U	Grosse Meister für kleine Hände, Bk. 2 (Kuranda)
		U	Old Masters for Young Pianists, Bk. 2 (Kuranda)
	Fantasia in A Minor	O	Piano Music for Young Wolfgang (No. 23)
	Fantasia in D Minor	O	Piano Music for Young Wolfgang (No. 21)
	Gavotte in D	Sch	Notebook for Wolfgang (No. 23)
	Gigue in D	O	Piano Music for Young Wolfgang (No. 22)
	March in C		(No. 11)
	March in D		(No. 16)
	March in F	Sch	Notebook for Wolfgang (No. 30)
		O	Piano Music for Young Wolfgang (No. 14)
	March in F		(No. 18)
	Menuet in A Minor	Sch	Notebook for Wolfgang (No. 26)
	Menuet in B-flat		(No. 22)

Composer	Title	Publisher	Volume or Collection
MOZART, L. (cont.)	Menuet in C	U	Grosse Meister für kleine Hände, Bk. 2 (Kuranda)
		U	Old Masters for Young Pianists, Bk. 2
	Menuet in C	Sch	Notebook for Wolfgang (No. 32)
	Menuet in C Minor		(No. 31)
	Menuet in F		(No. 18)
	Passepied in D		(No. 20)
	Polonaise in A		(No. 25)
	Polonaise in C		(No. 15)
	Polonaise in C	O	Piano Music for Young Wolfgang (No. 10)
	Polonaise in F	He	Nannerl Mozart's Piano Book (Kreutzer)
	Presto in A		
	Scherzo in C	O	Piano Music for Young Wolfgang (No. 20)
	Scherzo in F	He	Nannerl Mozart's Piano Book (Kreutzer)
		Sch	Notebook for Nannerl (No. 13)
MOZART, W. A. (1756-1791)	Adagio in C (From Viennese Sonatina No. 6)	Sch MMC GS He	Viennese Sonatinas
		CF	Road to Piano Artistry, Vol. VI (Scionti)
		K	Easy Compositions of Mozart and Beethoven
	Allegretto in C	Sch	The Young Mozart
	Andante in B-flat		
	Andante in F (K 6)	Sch	Notebook for Nannerl
	Andantino in E-flat (K 236)	GS	Introduction to Piano Classics, Vol. I (Mirovitch)
		He	A Treasury of Easy Classics
		P	Mozart Klavierstücke (Urtext)
	Contredanse in B-flat (K 15gg)	Co	The Classic Dances (Goldberger)
	Contredanse (K 15h)	Co	The Classic Dances (Goldberger)

	Easy Dances
	  1. Entrée
	  2. Cache-cache
	  3. Idyll
	  4. Gavotte joyeuse
	  6. Gavotte gracieuse
	  7. Pantomime
	  9. Gavotte
	10. Finale
	11. Minuetto in G
	12. Allegro
	13. Minuetto in F
	14. Andantino
	15. Minuetto in F
		Sch	A Little Book of Easy Dances

Composer	Title	Publisher	Volume or Collection
MOZART, W. A. (cont.)	German Dance (K 602)	Su	Piano Literature of the 17th, 18th and 19th Centuries, Bk. 3 (Clark)
	Kontretanz in F	Sch	The Young Mozart
	Menuetto in C (From Viennese Sonatina No. 1)	Sch	Six Viennese Sonatinas
		MMC	
		He	
		GS	
		CF	Road to Piano Artistry, Vol. III (Scionti)
		B	Hours with the Masters, Bk. II
		Su	Piano Literature of the 17th, 18th and 19th Centuries, Bk. 3 (Clark)
	Menuet in D (K 7)	Sch	Notebook for Nannerl
	Menuet in D (K 94)	K	Easy Compositions of Mozart and Beethoven
		Su	Piano Literature of the 17th, 18th and 19th Centuries, Bk. 4a (Clark)
	Menuett in F (K 4)	K	Easy Compositions of Mozart and Beethoven (No. 3)
		K	Mozart, Easy Compositions for Piano (No. 7)
		BMC	Mozart's First Five Compositions
		Sch	Notebook for Nannerl
		He	A Treasury of Easy Classics (Abrams)
		Co	The Classic Dances (Goldberger)
	Menuett in G	Sch	The Young Mozart (pg. 7)
		WR	Rediscovered Classics, Bk. 2
	Minuet in A (K 15ik)	Co	The Classic Dances (Goldberger)
	Minuet in C (K 15f)		
	Minuet in F (K 15m)		
	Minuet in G (K 15y)		
	Minuet in E-flat (K 15ee)		
	Presto	K	Mozart, Easy Compositions for Piano (No. 9)
	(Allegro in B-flat)	Co	The Solo Book, Vol. III (Zeetlin and Goldberger)
	Rondo in F	Sch	The Young Mozart
	Siziliano in D Minor		
	Sonatina in C	He	Little Treasury of Sonatinas, Bk. II
	Three Waltzes (K 600)	PP	Hundred Best Short Classics, Bk. 1
	Waltzes (K 600, 602, 605)	U	Twelve Waltzes
		P	German Dances
		Sch	Fifteen Waltzes (Frey)
	Waltz, K 602, No. 2 (German Dance)	Su	Piano Literature of the 17th, 18th and 19th Centuries, Bk. 4A (Clark)
	Waltz, K 605, No. 3 (German Dance)		

Composer	Title	Publisher	Volume or Collection
MOZART, W. A. (cont.)	Waltz in D	WR	Rediscovered Classics, Bk. 3 (Henderson)
MUFFAT, J. T. (1690-1770)	Menuet mit Jagdhörnern	U	Grosse Meister für kleine Hände, Bk. 2
MURCHHAUSER, F. (1663-1738)	Christmas Song	He	A Little Treasury of Classics, Bk. I (Lambert)
	Pastoral Air	BH	Airs and Dances, Bk. I (Dorolle)
NEEFE, C. G. (1748-1798)	Arioso in G	Sch GS	Simple Short Piano Pieces Introduction to Piano Classics, Bk. I (Mirovitch)
	Minuetto in C	Sch	Menuetten fürs Clavier
NICHELMANN, C. (1717-1762)	Polonaise in A	Sch	Clavierstücke für Anfänger
PASQUINI, B. (1637-1710)	Pastorale	BH	Airs and Dances, Bk. I
	Da Una Canzone Francese	K	Easy Pieces from Old Italian Masters
PURCELL, D. (1660-1717)	Air In D	H	Contemporaries of Purcell
PURCELL, H. (1658-1695)	Gavotte in G	H B WR	Contemporaries of Purcell Hours with the Masters, Bk. II Rediscovered Classics, Bk. 3
	Hornpipe in D (From D Major Suite VI)	BMC	Purcell-Arne Album
	Jig in G Minor	GS	Introduction to Piano Classics, Vol. I (Mirovitch)
	Minuet in G (From Suite in G, No. I)	PP BMC He A WR	Hundred Best Short Classics, Bk. I Purcell-Arne Album A Little Treasury of Classics, Bk. III (Lambert) Beringer's School of Easy Classics: Old English and French Masters Rediscovered Classics, Bk. I
	Riggadoon (From Suite in C, No. V) (Rigadon)	BMC BH	Purcell-Arne Album From Ancient to Modern
	Siciliano in G Minor (From Suite in G Minor No. II)	BH BMC A	Airs and Dances, Bk. I (Dorolle) Purcell-Arne Album Beringer's School of Easy Classics: Old English and French Masters
	Trumpet Tune II	GS WR	Introduction to Piano Classics, Vol. I (Mirovitch) Rediscovered Classics, (Henderson), Bk. I

Composer	Title	Publisher	Volume or Collection
RAMEAU, J. P. (1683-1764)	Le Lardon	BH	Airs and Dances, Bk. II (Dorolle)
	Minuet in C	He	A Little Treasury of Classics, Bk. I (Lambert)
	Minuet en Rondeau	BH	Airs and Dances, Bk. I (Dorolle)
	Minuet in G Minor	U	Old Masters for Young Pianists (Kuranda) Bk. I
		U	Grosse Meister für kleine Hände, Bk. 1 (Kuranda)
	Old French Dance	SG	Classics from the 17th and 18th Centuries
REICHARDT, J. F. (1752-1814)	Allegretto in A	Sch	Simple Short Piano Pieces
	Un poco presto e scher- zando in D		
ROLLE, J. H. (1718-1785)	Minuet in B-flat	Sch	Simple Short Piano Pieces
ROSSI, M. (? -1660)	Andantino	K	Easy Pieces from Old Italian Masters
RUDORF, C. F. (2nd half of 18th Century)	Polonaise in F	Sch	Clavierstücke für Anfänger
SCARLATTI, D. (1685-1757)	Allegro in G Minor	He	A Little Treasury of Classics, Bk. IV (Lambert)
	Aria	Co	The Solo Book, Vol. III (Zeetlin and Goldberger)
	Giga in D Minor	He	A Treasury of Easy Classics (Abrams)
	Larghetto in D Minor		
SCHMIEDT, S. (1756-1799)	Vivace in G	Sch GS	Simple Short Piano Pieces Introduction to Piano Classics, Vol. II (Mirovitch)
STÖLZEL, G. (1690-1749)	Air italien	P	Contemporaries of Telemann
	Bourrée in G Minor		
TELEMANN, G. P. (1681-1767)	Gigue à l'Angloise	K	The Direct Path (Herrmann)
	Gigue	Co	The Solo Book, Vol. III (Zeetlin and Goldberger)
	Loure in A Minor	P	Contemporaries of Telemann
	Menuett (From A Minor Suite)		
TÜRK, D. G. (TUERK) (1750-1813)	Climbing	He	A Little Treasury of Classics, Bk. III (Lambert)
	Kleine Sonate	Sch	Clavier Sonatinen (Kreutz)

Composer	Title	Publisher	Volume or Collection
TÜRK, D. G. (TUERK) (cont.)	Allegro ma non tanto Larghetto con tenerezza Poco allegro		
	The Gazelle	CF	Road to Piano Artistry, Vol. II (Scionti)
	Twenty Six Selected Pieces	K NVK	Türk: Forty-nine Pieces for Beginners Kleine Handstücke; Türk
	23. Sadness		
	24. Climbing		
	25. Consonants		
	26. Carefree		
	27. Mourning		
	28. Sing and Swing		
	29. The Master		
	30. Happy Memory		
	31. Stately Dance		
	32. Worry		
	33. Sicilienne		
	34. The Actor		
	35. Trio		
	36. Chorale		
	37. Etude		
	38. Variation		
	39. The Drama		
	40. Twirling (Rondino)	GS	Early Classics for the Piano (Mirovitch)
	41. Trumpets		
	42. Bad Temper		
	43. Variety		
	44. Violin and Piano		
	45. Canon		
	46. Grave		
	47. Left Hand Study		
	49. Fifth Finger		
UHDE, J. O. (1725-1766)	Tempo di Minuetto in C	Sch	Clavierstucke für Anfänger
VANHALL, J. B. (1739-1813)	Aria in B-flat (Cantabile in B-flat)	GS Sch	Introduction to Piano Classics, Vol. II (Mirovitch) Simple Short Piano Pieces
	Minuetto in G	GS Sch	Introduction to Piano Classics, Vol. II (Mirovitch) Simple Short Piano Pieces
WAGENSEIL, G. (1715-1777)	Allegro in F	U	Grosse Meister für kleine Hände, Bk. 2
	Minuet in F	SG	Classics of the Seventeenth and Eighteenth Centuries (Tapper)
WITTHAUER, J. G. (1750-1802)	Allegro scherzando in G Polonaise in D Poco vivace in A	Sch	Clavierstücke für Anfänger

Composer	Title	Publisher	Volume or Collection
ZIPOLI, D. (1675-1726)	Minuet, D Minor	K	Bach and His Contemporaries
	Sarabande	K	Easy Pieces for the Piano from Old Italian Masters

MUSIC OF THE NINETEENTH CENTURY

Composer	Title	Publisher	Volume or Collection
BEETHOVEN, L. van (1770-1827)	Allemande in A	Sch P	Kleine Tänze (Frey) (No. 5) Ecossaisen und Deutsche Tanze (No. 8)
	Allemande in E-flat	Sch P	Kleine Tänze (Frey) (No. 9) Ecossaisen und Deutsche Tanze (No. 5)
	Allemande in G	Sch P	Kleine Tänze (Frey) (No. 14) Ecossaisen und Deutsche Tanze (No. 6)
	Country Dance in D	Su	Piano Literature of the 16th, 17th and 18th Centuries, Bk. 5b (Clark)
	Country Dance in D	Sch H	Kleine Tänze (Frey) (No. 3) Easiest Original Pieces (No. 2)
	Country Dance in D	Sch Co	Kleine Tänze (Frey) (No. 11) Mozart-Beethoven, The Classic Dances
	(Country Dance I)	GS	Master Series for the Young
	(Country Dance I)	CF	Road to Piano Artistry, Vol. I (Scionti)
	Country Dance in D Minor	Sch	Kleine Tänze (Frey) (No. 6)
	Country Dance in D Minor	H	Easiest Original Pieces (No. 3)
	Für Elise	GS GS GS B	Published Separately Master Series for the Young Thirty-two Sonatinas and Rondos Hours with the Masters, Bk. III
	German Dances (Complete)	K	Six German Dances by Ludwig van Beethoven
	German Dance in C	P Su	Ecossaises und Deutsch Tänze (No. 1) Piano Literature of the 17th, 18th and 19th Centuries, Bk. 3
	German Dance in G	He	A Little Treasury of Classics, Bk. 1 (Lambert)
	Gertrude's Dream Waltz	GS	Published Separately
	Ländrer in E-flat	Sch	Kleine Tänze (Frey) (No. 18)
	Menuett in A		(No. 20)
	Menuett in B-flat		(No. 16)
	Menuett in B-flat (Minuet II)	H	(No. 13) Easiest Original Classics
	Menuett in E-flat	Sch	Kleine Tänze (Frey) (No. 10)
	Menuett in E-flat		(No. 17)
	Menuett in E-flat	GS	Master Series for the Young
	Menuett in G	Sch H	Kleine Tänze (Frey) (No. 4) Easiest Original Pieces

Composer	Title	Publisher	Volume or Collection
BEETHOVEN, L. van (cont.)		GS	Master Series for the Young
	(Minuet II)	Co	Mozart-Beethoven, The Classic Dances
	Seven Country Dances	Co	Mozart-Beethoven, The Classic Dances
	Six Minuets	BH	From Ancient to Modern (Rowley)
	Sonatina in F	P	Sonatinen Vorstufe, Vol. II
	Allegro assai	P	Beethoven Sonatinas
	Rondo	K	
		P	Sonatinen Album, Vol. II
		WR	Rediscovered Classics, Bk. I
		CF	Road to Piano Artistry, Vol. III (Scionti)
	Sonatina in G	P	Sonatinen Vorstufe, Vol. I
	Moderato	P	Beethoven Sonatinas
	Romanza	K	
		P	Sonatinen Album, Vol. II
		PP	Hundred Best Short Classics, Bk. I
		CF	Road to Piano Artistry, Vol. I (Scionti)
		Su	Piano Literature of the 17th, 18th and 19th Centuries, Bk. 2 (Clark)
	Twelve German Dances	P	Ecossaises und Deutsch Tänze
	Twelve German Dances	Co	Mozart-Beethoven, The Classic Dances
	Viennese Waltz in B-flat	Sch	Kleine Tänze (Frey) (No. 8)
	Viennese Waltz in D		(No. 19)
	Viennese Waltz in E-flat		(No. 15)
BERTINI, D. (1798-1876)	Allegretto	BH	From Ancient to Modern (Rowley)
	Andante in G (From Petits Morceaux)	P	Sonatinen Vorstufe, Vol. II, (No. 47)
BURGMÜLLER, N. (1810-1836)	Confidence	CF	Road to Piano Artistry, Vol. II (Scionti)
	L'Adieu (The Farewell)	GS	Twenty-five Easy and Progressive Studies, Op. 100
		He	
		Wo	
	La Chevaleresque (Spirit of Chivalry)	GS	Twenty-five Easy and Progressive Studies, Op. 100
		He	
		Wo	
	La Pastorale	GS	Twenty-five Easy and Progressive Studies, Op. 100
		He	
		Wo	
		CF	Road to Piano Artistry, Vol. I (Scionti)
	La petite reunion (The Little Party)	GS	Twenty-five Easy and Progressive Studies, Op. 100
		He	
		Wo	
	La Styrienne		

Composer	Title	Publisher	Volume or Collection
BURGMÜLLER, N. (cont.)	Le Retour (The Return)		
CHOPIN, F. (1810-1849)	Prelude in A, Op. 28	K	Chopin Preludes, Op. 28 (No. 7)
		PMP	
		P	
		GS	
		GS	Master Series for the Young
		H	Easiest Original Pieces
		PP	Hundred Best Short Classics, Bk. IV
		WR	Rediscovered Classics, Bk. 4 (Henderson)
	Prelude in C Minor, Op. 28	K	Chopin Preludes, Op. 28, (No. 20)
		PMP	
		P	
		GS	
		GS	Master Series for the Young
		H	Easiest Original Pieces
		PP	Hundred Best Short Classics, Bk. IV
		WR	Rediscovered Classics, Bk. 4 (Henderson)
CLEMENTI, M. (1752-1832)	Air Suisse, From Sonatina, Op. 36, No. 4	GS	Six Sonatinas, Op. 36, Clementi
		P	
		GS	Album of Sonatinas
		P	Sonatinen Album, Vol. I
		GS	Thirty-two Sonatinas and Rondos
	Andante con espressione, From Sonatina Op. 36, No. 4	GS	Six Sonatinas, Op. 36: Clementi
		P	
		GS	Album of Sonatinas
		P	Sonatinen Album, Vol. I
		WR	Rediscovered Classics, Bk. I (Henderson)
		GS	Thirty-two Sonatinas and Rondos
		B	Hours with the Masters, Bk. I
		CF	Road to Piano Artistry, Vol. V (Scionti)
	Sonatina in C, Op. 36, No. 1	GS	Six Sonatinas and Rondos
	Spiritoso	GS	Thirty-two Sonatinas and Rondos
	Andante	P	Sonatinen Album, Vol. I
	Vivace	GS	Album of Sonatinas
		P	Six Sonatinas, Op. 36: Clementi
		Su	Piano Literature of the 17th, 18th and 19th Centuries, Bk. 3 (Clark)
	Sonatina in G, Op. 36, No. 2	GS	Six Sonatinas, Op. 36: Clementi
	Allegretto	P	
	Allegretto	P	Sonatinen Album, Vol. I
	Allegro	GS	Album of Sonatinas
		GS	Thirty-two Sonatinas and Rondos
	Sonatina in F, Op. 38, No. 3	P	Sonatinen Album, Vol. II
	Allegro	GS	Selected Sonatinas, Bk. I
	Allegretto		
	Waltz in G	P	Sonatinen Vorstufe, Vol. I

Composer	Title	Publisher	Volume or Collection
DIABELLI, A. (1781-1858)	Rondino in C	WR	Rediscovered Classics, Bk. 1 (Henderson)
GADE, N. (1817-1890)	Boy's Merry-Go-Round, Op. 36, No. 4	GS	Selected Piano Solos by Romantic Composers, Bk. I Published Separately

	The Children's Christmas Eve
	  1. The Christmas Bells
	  2. Christmas Song
	  3. The Christmas Tree
	  4. Boy's Merry-Go-Round
	  5. Dance of Little Girls
	  6. Good Night
		K
		K
			The Children's Christmas Eve, Op. 36
			Published Separately

GRIEG, E. (1843-1907)	Albumleaf, Op. 12, No. 7	P GS GS GS He GS	Lyrical Pieces, Op. 12, Bk. 1 Lyrical Pieces, Op. 12 Grieg: Forty-five Selected Compositions, Bk. I Master Series for the Young A Little Treasury of Classics, Bk. IV (Lambert) Published Separately
	Arietta, Op. 12, No. 1	P GS K	Lyrical Pieces, Op. 12, Bk. 1 Lyrical Pieces, Op. 12
	Grandmother's Minuet, Op. 68, No. 2	P GS GS GS GS	Lyrical Pieces, Op. 68, Bk. 9 Lyrical Pieces, Op. 68 Grieg: Forty-five Selected Compositions, Bk. I Master Series for the Young Published Separately
	Patriotic Song, Op. 12, No. 8	P GS K GS GS Su	Lyrical Pieces, Op. 12, Bk. 1 Lyrical Pieces, Op. 12 Master Series for the Young Published Separately Piano Literature of the 17th, 18th and 19th Centuries, Bk. 4b (Clark)
	Walzer, Op. 12, No. 2	P GS K GS GS He Su GS	Lyrical Pieces, Op. 12, Bk. 1 Lyrical Pieces, Op. 12 Master Series for the Young Grieg: Forty-five Selected Compositions, Bk. I A Treasury of Easy Classics (Abrams) Piano Literature of the 17th, 18th and 19th Centuries, Bk. 4b (Clark) Published Separately

Composer	Title	Publisher	Volume or Collection
GRIEG, E. (cont.)	Watchman's Song, Op. 12, No. 3	P	Lyrical Pieces, Op. 12, Bk. 1
		GS	Lyrical Pieces, Op. 12
		K	
		GS	Grieg: Forty-five Selected Compositions, Bk. I
		GS	Master Series for the Young
		Su	Piano Literature of the 17th, 18th and 19th Centuries, Bk. 5b (Clark)
		Su	Published Separately
GURLITT, C. (1820-1901)	Album Leaves 2. Morning Prayer 14. Valse Noble 15. Loss	GS	Album Leaves for the Young, Op. 101
	Buds and Blossoms, Op. 107, No. 1	GS	Selected Piano Solos by Romantic Composers, Bk. II
	From, Op. 183, Nos. 3, 4, 5, 9, 10	BH	By The Fireside, Op. 183
	Impromptu, Op. 224, No. 5	B	Hours with the Masters, Bk. II
	In The Church, Op. 140, No. 12	GS	Selected Compositions by Romantic Composers, Bk. I
	Ländler, Op. 130, No. 8		
	Melodious Studies 4. March Violets 7. Old and Young 8. Pleasures of the Chase 9. A New Start 10. Patriotic Song 11. March 21. Dance of the Elves 23. Impatience	GS	Twenty-four Melodious Studies, Op. 131
	Minuet, Op. 224, No. 4	B	Hours with the Masters, Bk. II
HELLER, S. (1813-1888)	Selections from Op. 45 1. The Brook 5. The Maypole 7. Determination 8. Barcarolle 9. Heavenly Voices 10. Evening Prayer 14. Sailor's Song 16. Il Penseroso 18. Impatience	R GS K P	Twenty-five Studies for Piano, Op. 45
	Selections from Op. 46 2. Village Bells 3. In a Canoe 6. Gentle Caresses 7. Tarantelle	R GS K P	Thirty Studies for Piano, Op. 46

Composer	Title	Publisher	Volume or Collection
HELLER, S. (cont.)	11. Moonbeams on the River		
	22. The Court Dance		
	Selections from Op. 47	R	Twenty-five Studies for Piano, Op. 47
	1. Helter Skelter	GS	
	2. The Babbling Brook	K	
	4. Pleasant Thoughts	P	
	5. On the Alert		
	6. The Windmill		
	7. The Horse Race		
	9. The Sailboat		
	10. Sounds of the Valley		
	11. Pastoral		
	12. Imps at Play		
	13. The Coach		
	14. Barcarolle		
	15. Claire de Lune		
	16. Joyous Meeting		
	17. Butterflies		
	19. A Memento		
	21. Romance		
	23. Story Told at Twilight		
	A Memento, Op. 47, No. 19 (Berceuse)	GS	Fifty Selected Studies: Heller (No. 3)
		PP	Hundred Best Short Classics, Bk. I
	Butterflies, Op. 47, No. 17	GS	Fifty Selected Studies: Heller (No. 4)
	Celestial Voices, Op. 45, No. 9	GS	Selected Piano Solos by Romantic Composers, Bk. I
		GS	Fifty Selected Studies: Heller (No. 21)
	Chanson (Romance) Op. 47, No. 21	WR	Rediscovered Classics, Bk. 2 (Henderson)
	Curious Story, Op. 138, No. 9	GS	Published Separately
		CF	Road to Piano Artistry, Vol. III (Scionti)
	Determination, Op. 45, No. 7	GS	Fifty Selected Studies: Heller (No. 18)
		GS	Selected Piano Solos by Romantic Composers, Bk. II
	Etude, Op. 45, No. 1 (Etude in C)	H	Contemporaries of Schumann
		B	Hours with the Masters, Bk. III
		GS	Fifty Selected Studies: Heller (No. 15)
	Etude in B Minor	CF	Road to Piano Artistry, Vol. III (Scionti)
	Evening Prayer, Op. 45, No. 10	GS	Fifty Selected Studies: Heller (No. 22)
	Gentle Caresses, Op. 46, No. 6		(No. 34)
	Gypsies II	CF	Road to Piano Artistry, Vol. II (Scionti)
	Il Penseroso, Op. 45, No. 16	GS	Published Separately
		GS	Fifty Selected Studies: Heller (No. 25)

Composer	Title	Publisher	Volume or Collection
HELLER, S. (cont.)	Impatience, Op. 45, No. 18	GS GS	Published Separately Fifty Selected Studies: Heller (No. 26)
	In a Canoe, Op. 46, No. 3	GS	Fifty Selected Studies: Heller (No. 32)
	In a Thoughtful Mood, Op. 47, No. 1	WR	Rediscovered Classics, Bk. 1 (Henderson)
	In the Highlands of Scotland (Pastorale), Op. 47, No. 11	He	A Little Treasury of Classics, Bk. II (Lambert)
	Little Caprice	CF	Road to Piano Artistry, Vol. II (Scionti)
	Little Etude, Op. 47, No. 1	CF	Road to Piano Artistry, Vol. I (Scionti)
	Moonbeams on the River, Op. 46, No. 11	GS	Fifty Selected Studies: Heller (No. 38)
	On the Alert, Op. 47, No. 5		(No. 6)
	Sailor's Song, Op. 45, No. 14	GS GS	Published Separately Fifty Selected Studies: Heller (No. 23) Selected Piano Solos by Romantic Composers, Bk. II
	Study in E, Op. 47, No. 16	GS GS	Selected Piano Solos by Romantic Composers, Bk. II Fifty Selected Studies: Heller (No. 13)
	Study in G, Op. 47, No. 4 (Pleasant Thoughts)	GS GS	Selected Piano Solos by Romantic Composers, Bk. I Fifty Selected Studies: Heller (No. 5)
	Sounds of the Valley, Op. 47, No. 10	GS	Fifty Selected Studies: Heller (No. 8)
	Story at Twilight, Op. 47, No. 23 (Song Without Words)	 WR	(No. 12) Rediscovered Classics, Bk. 3 (Henderson)
	Tarantelle, Op. 46, No. 7	GS CF PP He	Fifty Selected Studies: Heller (No. 35) Road to Piano Artistry, Vol. IV (Scionti) Hundred Best Short Classics, Bk. II A Treasury of Easy Classics (Abrams)
	(Etude in E Minor) (Petite Tarantelle)	B GS	Hours with the Masters, Bk. III Published Separately
	The Babbling Brook, Op. 47, No. 2	GS	Fifty Selected Studies: Heller (No. 1)
	The Coach, Op. 47, No. 13		(No. 10)
	The Maypole, Op. 45, No. 5		(No. 20)
	The Sailboat, Op. 47, No. 9		(No. 7)
	The Windmill, Op. 47, No. 6		(No. 9)

Composer	Title	Publisher	Volume or Collection
KUHLAU, F. (1786-1832)	Sonatina in C, Op. 55, No. 1	P	Sonatinen Album, Vol. I
		GS	Sonatina Album
	Allegro	GS	Kuhlau Sonatinas, Bk. I
	Vivace	GS	Thirty-two Sonatinas and Rondos
		He	Little Treasury of Sonatinas, Bk. II
	Sonatina in G, Op. 55, No. 2	P	Sonatinen Album, Vol. I
		GS	Sonatina Album
	Allegretto	GS	Kuhlau Sonatinas, Bk. I
	Cantabile	GS	Thirty-two Sonatinas and Rondos
	Allegro	CF	Road to Piano Artistry, Vol. I (Scionti)
KULLAK, T. (1818-1882)	Boating on the Lake (Barcarolle), Op. 62, No. 7	CF	Road to Piano Artistry, Vol. I (Scionti)
	Scenes From Childhood, Op. 62	GS	Scenes From Childhood
		K	
	1. Once Upon A Time		
	2. The Clock		
	3. Sunday Morning		
	4. On The Play-Ground		
	5. Little Cradle Song		
	6. Dance On The Lawn (Dance on the Green)	WR	Rediscovered Classics, Bk. 2 (Henderson)
	7. Barcarolle		
	8. Grand Parade		
	9. The Birdie's Death		
	10. The Mill By The Brook		
	11. Skating		
	12. Evening Bell		
	Scenes From Childhood, Op. 81	GS	Scenes From Childhood
	1. Child's Prayer		
	2. The Little Wanderer		
	3. Grandmother Tells A Ghost Story		
	4. Opening of the Children's Party (Polonaise)	WR	Rediscovered Classics, Bk. 2 (Henderson)
	5. Loving Soul and Pure Heart Gay		
	6. The Race		
	7. The Angels in the Dream		
	8. The Nightingale		

Composer	Title	Publisher	Volume or Collection
KULLAK, T. (cont.)	9. Spinning-Song 10. The Ghost in the Fireplace 11. The Little Hunters 12. The Little Rope-Dancer		
	The Clock, Op. 62, No. 2	CF GS	Road to Piano Artistry, Vol. VI (Scionti) Selected Compositions by Romantic Composers, Bk. I
	The Ghost in the Fireplace, Op. 81, No. 10	GS GS	Selected Compositions by Romantic Composers, Bk. I Published Separately
	The Mill By The Brook, Op. 62, No. 10	CF	Road to Piano Artistry, Vol. V (Scionti)
	The Nightingale, Op. 81, No. 8	GS	Selected Compositions by Romantic Composers, Bk. I
	The Race, Op. 81, No. 6		
	Skating, Op. 62, No. 11	GS	Published Separately
LIADOV, A. (1855-1914)	Four Russian Folk Songs 1. On The Steppes 2. A Day At The Fair 3. Sleep My Child 4. I Danced With A Mosquito	L L Co	Four Russian Folk Songs (Siloti) The Student Pianist, Vol. I (Mirovitch) The Solo Book, Vol. III (Zeetlin and berger)
MACDOWELL, E. (1861-1908)	An Old Garden, Op. 62, No. 1	GS K	New England Idylls, Op. 62
	Song, Op. 55, No. 5	GS	Sea Pieces, Op. 55
	To A Wild Rose, Op. 51, No. 1	K M GS Sch Su	Woodland Sketches, Op. 51 Piano Literature of the 17th, 18th and 19th Centuries, Bk. 5b (Clark)
SCHUBERT, F. (1797-1828)	Ecossaises, Op. 33	P GS	Schubert Dances
	Ecossaise, Op. 18a, No. 3	Co A H	The Solo Book, Vol. III (Zeetlin and Goldberger) Beringer's School of Easy Classics: Schubert Easiest Original Pieces
	Ecossaise in B Minor, Op. 33	B	Hours With the Masters, Bk. III
	Ecossaise in D, No. 5 (From Five Ecossaises)	A	Beringer's School of Easy Classics: Schubert

Composer	Title	Publisher	Volume or Collection
SCHUMANN, R. (1810-1856)	First Loss, Op. 68, No. 16	P	Album for the Young, Op. 68
		K	
		Co	
		GS	
		GS	Published Separately
		GS	Master Series for the Young
		He	A Treasury of Easy Classics (Abrams)
		Su	Piano Literature of the 17th, 18th and 19th Centuries, Bk. 3 (Clark)
	Folk Song, Op. 68, No. 9	P	Album for the Young, Op. 68
		K	
		Co	
		GS	
		GS	Selected Piano Solos by Romantic Composers, Bk. II
		A	Beringer's School of Easy Classics: Schumann
	Harvest Song, Op. 68, No. 24	P	Album for the Young, Op. 68
		K	
		Co	
		GS	
	Hunting Song, Op. 68, No. 7	P	Album for the Young, Op. 68
		K	
		Co	
		GS	
		GS	Master Series for the Young
		B	Hours with the Masters, Bk. II
		He	A Little Treasury of Classics, Bk. IV (Lambert)
		Su	Piano Literature of the 17th, 18th and 19th Centuries, Bk. 4b (Clark)
	Knight Rupert, Op. 68, No. 12	P	Album for the Young, Op. 68
		K	
		Co	
		GS	
		GS	Selected Piano Solos by Romantic Composers, Bk. I
		A	Beringer's School of Easy Classics: Schumann
		CF	Road to Piano Artistry, Vol. IV (Scionti)
		GS	Published Separately
	Little Romance, Op. 68, No. 19	P	Album for the Young, Op. 68
		K	
		Co	
		GS	
		GS	Master Series for the Young
	Little Study, Op. 68, No. 14	P	Album for the Young, Op. 68
		K	
		Co	
		GS	
		GS	Master Series for the Young

Composer	Title	Publisher	Volume or Collection
SCHUMANN, R. (cont.)		GS	Selected Piano Solos by Romantic Composers, Bk. I
		P	Sonatinen Album, Vol. II
	Poor Orphan, Op. 68, No. 6	P	Album for the Young, Op. 68
		K	
		Co	
		GS	
		A	Beringer's School of Easy Classics: Schumann
		B	Hours with the Masters, Bk. II
		PP	Hundred Best Short Classics, Bk. I
		GS	Selected Piano Solos by Romantic Composers, Bk. II
	Reaper's Song, Op. 68, No. 18	P	Album for the Young, Op. 68
		K	
		Co	
		GS	
		A	Beringer's School of Easy Classics: Schumann
		B	Hours with the Masters, Bk. II
		GS	Master Series for the Young
		CF	Road to Piano Artistry, Vol. II (Scionti)
		P	Sonatinen Vorstufe, Vol. I
	Rustic Song, Op. 68, No. 20	P	Album for the Young, Op. 68
		K	
		Co	
		GS	
		B	Hours with the Masters, Bk. III
		Su	Piano Literature of the 17th, 18th and 19th Centuries, Bk. 5b (Clark)
		GS	Published Separately
	Sicilienne, Op. 68, No. 11	P	Album for the Young, Op. 68
		K	
		Co	
		GS	
		A	Beringer's School of Easy Classics: Schumann
		GS	Selected Piano Solos by Romantic Composers, Bk. I
		GS	Published Separately
		Co	The Solo Book, Vol. III (Zeetlin and Goldberger)
		Su	Piano Literature of the 17th, 18th and 19th Centuries, Bk. 4b (Clark)
	The Rider's Story, Op. 68, No. 23	P	Album for the Young, Op. 68
		K	
		Co	
		GS	
		GS	Master Series for the Young
		GS	Selected Piano Solos by Romantic Composers, Bk. II
		GS	Published Separately

Composer	Title	Publisher	Volume or Collection
SCHUMANN, R. (cont.)	The Wild Horseman, Op. 68, No. 23	P	Album for the Young, Op. 68
		K	
		Co	
		GS	
		GS	Published Separately
		A	Beringer's School of Easy Classics: Schumann
		He	A Little Treasury of Classics, Bk. III (Lambert)
		GS	Master Series for the Young
		He	A Treasury of Easy Classics (Abrams)
		Su	Piano Literature of the 17th, 18th and 19th Centuries, Bk. 3 (Clark)
TSCHAIKOWSKY, P. (1840-1893)	At Church, Op. 39, No. 24	GS	Album for the Young, Op. 39
		P	
		GS	Master Series for the Young
	Farmer's Boy Playing on the Accordian, Op. 39, No. 12	GS	Album for the Young, Op. 39
		P	
		GS	Master Series for the Young
	Italian Song, Op. 39, No. 15	GS	Album for the Young, Op. 39
		P	
		GS	Master Series for the Young
		P	Sonatinen Album, Vol. II
	Mama, Op. 39, No. 4	GS	Album for the Young, Op. 39
		P	
	March of the Tin Soldiers, Op. 39, No. 5	GS	Album for the Young, Op. 39
		P	
		Su	Piano Literature of the 17th, 18th and 19th Centuries, Bk. 3 (Clark)
	Mazurka, Op. 39, No. 10	GS	Album for the Young, Op. 39
		P	
		GS	Master Series for the Young
		PP	Hundred Best Short Classics, Bk. II
		CF	Road to Piano Artistry, Vol. II (Scionti)
	Morning Prayer, Op. 39, No. 1	GS	Album for the Young, Op. 39
		P	
		GS	Master Series for the Young
		He	A Little Treasury of Classics, Bk. III (Lambert)
		GS	Selected Piano Solos by Romantic Composers, Bk. I
	Neopolitan Song, Op. 39, No. 18	GS	Album for the Young, Op. 39
		P	
		GS	Master Series for the Young
		GS	Selected Piano Solos by Romantic Composers, Bk. I
		Su	Piano Literature of the 17th, 18th and 19th Centuries, Bk. 5b (Clark)
	Russian Song, Op. 39, No. 11	GS	Album for the Young
		P	
		GS	Master Series for the Young

Composer	Title	Publisher	Volume or Collection
TSCHAIKOWSKY, P. (cont.)	Sweet Dreams, Op. 39, No. 21	GS P	Album for the Young, Op. 39
		GS	Master Series for the Young
		H	Contemporaries of Schumann
		H	Easiest Original Classics
		CF	Road to Piano Artistry, Vol. II (Scionti)
		He	A Treasury of Easy Classics (Abrams)
	Song of the Lark, Op. 39, No. 22	GS P	Album for the Young, Op. 39
		GS	Master Series for the Young
		CF	Road to Piano Artistry, Vol. VI (Scionti)
		GS	Selected Piano Solos by Romantic Composers, Bk. I
		GS	Published Separately
	The New Doll, Op. 39, No. 9	GS P	Album for the Young, Op. 39
		PP	Hundred Best Short Classics, Bk. I
	The Organgrinder, Op. 39, No. 23	GS P	Album for the Young, Op. 39
		GS	Master Series for the Young
		Co	The Solo Book, Vol. III (Zeetlin and Goldberger)
WEBER, C. (1786-1826)	German Dance	Co	The Solo Book, Vol. III (Zeetlin and Goldberger)
	German Waltz	He	Little Treasury of Classics, Bk. II
	Original Theme, Op. 9	GS	Master Series for the Young
	Waltz in G	He	A Little Treasury of Classics, Bk. III (Lambert)

Composer	Title	Publisher	Volume or Collection

ANTHEIL, GEORGE (1900-1958)	Suite for the Piano
	  1. Practice Hours
	     Are Long
	  2. In Spain with Mr.
	     Hemingway
	  3. Someday We'll Like
	     Stravinsky
		GS	Suite for the Piano

BADINGS, HENK (1907-)	Reihe kleiner Klavierstücke
	  1. Intrada
	  2. Siciliano
	  3. Ballo Gaio
	  4. Air
	  5. Rondo popolare
	  6. Menuet
	  7. Scherzo Pastorale
	  8. Rondo-Finale
		Sch	Reihe kleiner Klavierstücke

	From "Arcadia," Bk. 3, Nos. 5 and 9	Sch	Arcadia, Bk. 3
BARTÓK, BÉLA (1881-1945)	Dance Tune	BH K L MMC	For Children, Vol. I (No. 12) 42 Hungarian Folk Melodies (No. 12) Meet Modern Music, Pt. II
	Energy	BH K L MMC	For Children, Vol. I (No. 21) 42 Hungarian Folk Melodies, (No. 21) Meet Modern Music, Pt. II
	From "For Children," Vol. I, Nos. 12, 21, 23, 26, 28, 32, 33, 35-40	BH K	For Children, Vol. I
	From "For Children," Vol. II, Nos. 11, 18, 21, 22, 25, 26, 27, 29, 33, 34, 36, 37, 39, 40	BH K	For Children, Vol. II
	From "Hungarian Folk Melodies", Nos. 12, 21, 23, 26, 28, 30, 31, 34, 35, 37-40	L	42 Hungarian Folk Melodies (Same contents as "For Children," Vol. I except Nos. 25 and 31)

	From "Mikrokosmos," Vol. III
	    Merriment
	    Variations
		BH	Mikrokosmos, Vol. III

	From "Mikrokosmos," Vol. IV	BH	Mikrokosmos, Vol. IV

Composer	Title	Publisher	Volume or Collection
BARTÓK, BÉLA (cont.)	Melody in the Mist Nutturno		
	From "16 Pieces for Children," Nos. 9, 10, 11, 16	I	16 Pieces for Children (Contents selected from "For Children," Vol. I, and "Ten Easy Pieces")

	From "Ten Easy Pieces for Children"
	    Dedication
	    Flight
	    Sostenuto
	    Evening in the Country
	    Hungarian Folksong
	    Sunrise
		K	Ten Easy Pieces for Children

	Selections from "For Children," Vol. I
	    Folk Tune (No. 35 from "For Children"
	    Game (No. 21 from "For Children")
	    Drunkard's Song (No. 36 from "For Children")
	    Swineherd's Song (No. 37 from "For Children")
		Su	Contemporary Piano Literature, Bk. 5 (Clark)

	Teasing	BH Su	For Children, Vol. II (No. 18) Contemporary Piano Literature, Bk. 3 (Clark)
BARVINSKY (1888-)	Lullaby	W	Modern Russian Piano Music
	Round Dance	L Su	Children's Piano Pieces by Soviet Composers Musical Finds from the 20th Century (Podolsky)
	Mr. and Mrs. Beetle	W	Modern Russian Piano Music
	The Mouse and the Bear	W L	Modern Russian Piano Music Children's Piano Pieces by Soviet Composers
	The Little Mosquito	L	Children's Piano Pieces by Soviet Composers
	The Little Rabbit		
	The Little Sparrow		
	Mr. Rooster Threshes Wheat		
	Round Dance		
BLOCH, ERNEST (1880-1959)	Ten Pieces for Children	CF CF	Enfantines Published Separately

Composer	Title	Publisher	Volume or Collection
BLOCH, ERNEST (cont.)	1. Lullaby 2. The Joyous Party 3. With Mother 4. Elves 5. Joyous March 6. Melody 7. Pastorale 8. Rainy Day 9. Teasing 10. Dream		

BORTKIEWICZ, S. (1877-1952)	Nine Easy Piano Pieces, Op. 54
	  1. Russian Peasant Girl
	  2. The Cossack
	  3. The Spanish Dancer
	  4. The Tyrolese
	  5. The Gypsy
	  6. The Marchioness
	  7. The Chinaman
	  8. Teddy Bear
	  9. Harlequin
		AMP	Marionettes, Op. 54

BOWLES, PAUL (1910-)	Folk Preludes
	  3. Whar Did You Cum From
	  5. Cape Ann
	  6. Ole Tare River
	  7. Kentucky Moonshiner
		MMC	Folk Preludes

BRIDGE, FRANK (1844-1924)	Miniature Pastorals (Set I)
	  1. Allegretto con moto
	  2. Tempo di Valse
	  3. Allegretto ben moderato
		BH	Miniature Pastorals for Piano

CARVAJAL, ARMANDO (?)	Miniature	MMC	Meet Modern Music, Part II
	Tristess	MMC	Meet Modern Music, Part II

CASELLA, ALFREDO (1883-1947)	Children's Pieces
	  1. Preludio
	  6. Siciliano
		AMP	Eleven Children's Pieces

CASTRO, JOSÉ MARIA (1892-)	Vals Minatura	EAM	Published Separately
CASTRO, JUAN JOSÉ (1895-)	Bear Dance	CF	Published Separately
	Quasi Polka	EAM	Published Separately
CASTRO, WASHINGTON (1909-)	Arroro	EAM	Published Separately
	Companitas De Fiesta	EAM	Published Separately

Composer	Title	Publisher	Volume or Collection
COPLAND, AARON (1900-)	Down A Country Lane	BH	Published Separately
	Sunday Afternoon Music	CF	Masters Of Our Day; 18 Solos in the Contemporary Idiom
		CF	Published Separately
COWELL, HENRY (1897-)	The Irishman Dances	CF	Masters of Our Day; 18 Solos in the Contemporary Idiom
		CF	Published Separately
CRESTON, PAUL (1906-)	Five Little Dances　1. Rustic Dance　2. Languid Dance　3. Toy Dance　4. Pastoral Dance　5. Festive Dance	GS	Five Little Dances, Op. 24
DELUNE, LOUIS (1876-1940)	Cinq Morceaux Faciles	E	Cinq Morceaux Faciles Pour Piano
		E	Published Separately
	1. Automobile　2. Gracieusement　3. A dos d'Ane　4. Le chevrier qui passe　5. La Senorita Conchita		
DIAMOND, DAVID (1915-)	Album for the Young　Little March　Waltz　Happy-Go-Lucky　Tender Thoughts　A Gambol　Christmastide　Spring Song　The Sad Slant-Eyed Boy　Jostling Joe　The Day's End	EV	Album for the Young
ELWELL, HERBERT (1898-)	Bus Ride	CF	Published Separately
	Plaint	TP	Published Separately
	Tarantella	CF	Published Separately
FERNANDEZ, O. L. (1897-1948)	Yaya, The Doll　1. Dancing Yaya　2. Dreaming Yaya　3. Jumping Yaya	PI	Yaya, The Doll
FICHER, JACABO (1896-)	El Desfile (March in File)	EAM	Published Separately
FINNEY, ROSS LEE (1906-)	From "Inventions"　8. Reflections	Su	Inventions
		Su	Contemporary Piano Literature, Bk. 4 (Clark)
	9. Lonesome Song		

Composer	Title	Publisher	Volume or Collection
FINNEY, ROSS LEE (cont.)	10. Playing Tag		
	11. Uncertainty		
	12. Doubt		
	13. March		
	14. All Alone		
	15. Hopping	Su	Contemporary Piano Literature, Bk. 6 (Clark)
	16. Chatter		
	17. Swinging	Su	Contemporary Piano Literature, Bk. 6 (Clark)
	18. Walking		
	19. Mirrors		
	20. Double Mirrors (Mirrors)	Su	Contemporary Piano Literature, Bk. 5 (Clark)
	21. Night	Su	Contemporary Piano Literature, Bk. 6 (Clark)
	22. Song	Su	Contemporary Piano Literature, Bk. 5 (Clark)
	23. Running Around	Su	Contemporary Piano Literature, Bk. 6 (Clark)
	24. Shadows		
	25. Vacation	Su	Contemporary Piano Literature, Bk. 5 (Clark)
FREED, ISADORE (1900-1960)	Jeneral Jerry's Jolly Jugglers	CF	Masters of Our Day; 18 Solos in the Contemporary Idiom
		CF	Published Separately
	With Trumpets and Drums	CF	Published Separately
FULEIHAN, ANIS (1900-)	Short Pieces	So	Five Very Short Pieces for Talented Young Bipeds
	3. Sentimental Journey		
	4. Stealthy Tread		
	5. Brisk March		
GIANNEO, LUIS (1897-)	Caminito De Belén	EAM	Published Separately
	Music for Children	EAM	Musica Para Ninos
	2. The Juggler		
	5. Indian Flute		
	6. Argentine Rustic Dance		
	Villancico (Christmas Carol)	EAM	Published Separately
GLIÉRE, REINHOLD (1875-1926)	In a Monastary	SG	Russian Piano Classics
	Rondino in B Minor	WR	Rediscovered Classics, Bk. 2 (Henderson)
GOEDICKE, ALEXANDER (1877-)	A Gay Prank	L	The Student Pianist, Vol. I (Mirovitch)
	Butterflies	SG	Russian Piano Classics
	Gavotte	SG	Russian Piano Classics
	In a Quiet Mood	MMC	Meet Modern Music, Pt. I

Composer	Title	Publisher	Volume or Collection
GOEDICKE, ALEXANDER (cont.)	Slow Waltz	L	Children's Piano Pieces by Soviet Composers
GOOSSENS, EUGENE (1893-1962)	Bonzo's Dance	CF	Published Separately
	Pikki's Lament		
GREEN, RAY (1909-)	Four Pieces for Piano Solo 1. Pieces to Begin 2. March 3. Melody 4. Piece to End	AME	Pieces for Children
	Song Sonatina	AME	Published Separately
	Square Dance Sonatina		
GRETCHANINOFF, ALEXANDER (1864-1956)	Gouaches 1. At Joyful Work 2. In Solitude 3. Encounter	L	Gouaches, Op. 189
	Happy Meeting	Co	The Solo Book, Vol. 3 (Zeetlin and Goldberger)
	Holidays	MMC	Meet Modern Music, Pt. I
	Mommy		
	Six Pieces from "Album de Nina" 2. Chansonnette 4. Songerie 5. Marche 6. Mélodie Antique 8. Au crépuscule 10. En Promenade	E	Album de Nina, Op. 141
	Six Pieces from "A Child's Day" 5. Father and Mother 6. A Visit to Grandmother 7. Grandmother's Waltz 8. The Happy Return Home 9. Nurse's Tale 10. Bedtime	Sch	A Child's Day, Op. 109
HALFFTER, RUDOLFO (1905-)	Danza de Avila	CF	Published Separately
HANSON, HOWARD (1896-)	Dance of the Warriors Enchantment The Bell	CF	Masters of Our Day; 18 Solos in the Contemporary Idiom (also Published Separately)

Composer	Title	Publisher	Volume or Collection
HINDEMITH, PAUL (1895-1963)	Easy 5-Tone Pieces	Sch	Kleine Klaviermusik (Sing-Und Spiel-musiken, No. 4)
	1. Massig Schnell		
	2. Ruhig bewegt		
	3. Munter, Schnell Viertal		
	4. Lebhaft, sehr markiert		
	5. Schnell, Ganze Takte		
	6. Gemächlich		
	7. Schnell und Wild		
	8. Massig Schnell		
	9. Langsam, ruhig shreitend		
	10. Munter, zimlich lebhaft		
	11. Massig Schnell		
	12. Bewegt		
	Wir Bauen Eine Stadt	Sch	Wir Bauen Eine Stadt
	1. Marsch		
	2. Lied		
	3. Musikstück		
	4. Lied		
	5. Man spielt „Besuch"		
	6. Die Diebe kommen in der nacht		
HOVHANESS, ALAN (1911-)	Mystic Flute, Op. 22	P	Published Separately
KABALEVSKY, DMITRI (1904-)	A Cozy Waltz, Op. 39, No. 23	L Su	The Student Pianist, Vol. I (Mirovitch) Contemporary Piano Literature, Bk. 3 (Clark)
	(Slow Waltz)	I	24 Little Pieces for Children, Opus 39
	A Little Fairy Tale	L I	15 Pieces for Children, Op. 27 18 Pieces for Children, Op. 27
	A Sad Story	L	Children's Piano Pieces by Soviet Composers
	A Short Story	L	15 Pieces for Children, Op. 27
	Ballad	I	18 Pieces for Children, Op. 27
	Carefree, Op. 39, No. 22	L	The Student Pianist, Vol. I
	Dance	L	15 Pieces for Children, Op. 27 (No. 15)
	Dancing On The Lawn	L I Su	15 Pieces for Children, Op. 27 18 Pieces for Children, Op. 27 Contemporary Piano Literature, Bk. 4 (Clark)
	Etude	L I Su	15 Pieces for Children, Op. 27 18 Pieces for Children, Op. 27 Contemporary Piano Literature, Bk. 5 (Clark)
	Fairy Tale	I	18 Pieces for Children, Op. 27

Composer	Title	Publisher	Volume or Collection
KABALEVSKY, DMITRI (cont.)	Four Little Pieces, Op. 14 　1. The Drummer 　2. A Brisk Game 　3. In the Gymnasium 　　(The Game) 　4. Soldiers March	L W	Four Little Pieces, Op. 14 Modern Russian Piano Music
	Gay Journey	I	24 Little Pieces for Children, Op. 39
	Having Fun	L I	15 Pieces for Children, Op. 27 18 Pieces for Children, Op. 27
	Improvization	I	24 Little Pieces for Children, Op. 39
	Joking (A Little Joke)	I L L L Su	18 Pieces for Children, Op. 27 15 Pieces for Children, Op. 27 Children's Piano Pieces by Soviet Composers Published Separately Contemporary Piano Literature, Bk. 4 (Clark)
	Novelette, Op. 27	L Su	15 Pieces for Children, Op. 27 Contemporary Piano Literature, Bk. 5 (Clark)
	Novelette, Op. 39	I	24 Little Pieces for Children, Op. 39
	Old Dance	L I L	15 Pieces for Children, Op. 27 18 Pieces for Children, Op. 27 Children's Piano Pieces by Soviet Composers
	Rondino	I	18 Pieces for Children, Op. 27
	Scherzo	I L L Su	18 Pieces for Children, Op. 27 15 Pieces for Children, Op. 27 Children's Piano Pieces by Soviet Composers Contemporary Piano Literature, Bk. 5 (Clark)
	Selected Pieces 　　5. Alter Tanze 　　　(Old Dance) 　　9. Kleiner Scherz 　　　(A Little Joke) 　10. Scherzo 　11. Kriegerischer Tanz 　12. Ein Märchen 　　　(A Short Story) 　14. Novelle (Novelette, Op. 27) 　15. Etude in A Major 　16. Dance 　17. Dramatisches Fragment	P	Kabalevsky, Selected Piano Pieces for Children

Composer	Title	Publisher	Volume or Collection
KABALEVSKY, DMITRI (cont.)	Slow Waltz (A Cozy Waltz)	I Su	24 Little Pieces for Children, Op. 39 Contemporary Piano Literature, Bk. 3 (Clark)
	Soldier's Dance	I	18 Pieces for Children, Op. 27
	Sonatina	I L L Su	18 Pieces for Children, Op. 27 15 Pieces for Children, Op. 27 Published Separately Contemporary Piano Literature, Bk. 4 (Clark)
	The Clown, Op. 39, No. 20	L Su Co	The Student Pianist, Vol. I (Mirovitch) Musical Finds from the 20th Century (Podolsky) The Solo Book, Vol. III (Zeetlin and Goldberger)
	The Horseman	Su	Contemporary Piano Literature, Bk. 1 (Clark)
	Toccatina	L I Su	15 Pieces for Children, Op. 27 18 Pieces for Children, Op. 27 Contemporary Piano Literature, Bk. 4 (Clark)
	Waltz	I	18 Pieces for Children, Op. 27
KHACHATURIAN, ARAM (1903-)	Three Pieces from "Adventures of Ivan" 1. Ivan Sings 2. Ivan Can't Go Out Today 3. Ivan Is Ill	L	Adventures of Ivan (Mirovitch)
KODÁLY, ZOLTÁN (1882-)	From "Children's Dances" 4. Moderato cantabile 5. Allegro moderato, poco rubato 6. Vivace 7. Vivace quasi marcia 8. Friss 9. Allegro marcato 10. Allegretto leggiero 11. Vivace 12. Allegro comodo	BH	Children's Dances
MAYKAPAR, SAMUEL (1867-1938)	At the Blacksmith's, Op. 8, No. 5 (The Blacksmith)	MMC L	Meet Modern Music, Pt. II 18 Selected Pieces (Mirovitch)
	Ballad	L	18 Selected Pieces
	Dewdrops	L L	18 Selected Pieces The Student Pianist, Vol. I (Mirovitch)
	Gavotte	L	The Student Pianist, Vol. I (Mirovitch)
	Passing Fancy	L L	The Student Pianist, Vol. I (Mirovitch) 18 Selected Pieces

Composer	Title	Publisher	Volume or Collection
MAYKAPAR, SAMUEL (cont.)	Skating	L	18 Selected Pieces
	Student Piece	L	18 Selected Pieces
	The Little Shepherd	L	18 Selected Pieces
		L	The Student Pianist, Vol. I (Mirovitch)
	The Moth	L	The Student Pianist, Vol. I (Mirovitch)
		L	18 Selected Pieces
	The Music Box	L	The Student Pianist, Vol. I (Mirovitch)
	Toccatina	L	18 Selected Pieces
	Polka	L	18 Selected Pieces
	Variations	L	18 Selected Pieces
MENOTTI, GIAN-CARLO (1911-)	From "Poemetti" 2. Lullaby 3. Bells at Dawn 4. The Spinner 5. The Bagpipers 11. The Manger	R	Poemetti
MIASKOWSKY, NIKOLAI (1881-1951)	A Small Duet	L	Children's Piano Pieces by Soviet Composers
	Harvest Song, Op. 14, No. 8	W	Modern Russian Piano Music
	In Old Fashioned Style	L	Children's Piano Pieces by Soviet Composers
	In Waltz Style		
	Spring Mood		
MILHAUD, DARIUS (1892-)	Three Pieces from "The Child Loves" 1. Flowers 2. Candy 3. Toys	L	The Child Loves
MOORE, DOUGLAS (1893-)	Dance For A Holiday	TP	Published Separately
	Escolator	Su	Contemporary Piano Literature, Bk. 4 (Clark)
	The Princess and The Pea		
PERSICHETTI, VINCENT (1915-)	Serenade, Op. 2, No. 2 1. Tune 2. Strum 3. Pluck	EV	Serenade, Op. 2, No. 2
	From Opus 60 7. Humoresque 8. Fanfare 9. Interlude 13. Fugue 14. Gloria	EV	Little Piano Book, Op. 60

Composer	Title	Publisher	Volume or Collection

PINTO, OCTAVIO (1890-1950)	Children's Festival
	  1. Prelude
	  2. Menuet
	  3. Little March
	  4. Serenade
	  5. Playing Marbles
		GS	Children's Festival

PISK, PAUL (1893-)	From Old Mexicale	CF	Published Separately
POLDINI, EDWARD (1869-1957)	Dance of the Gnomes	GS	Published Separately
PONCE, MANUEL (1882-1948)	Elegy	PI	Published Separately
	Momento Doloroso	PI	Published Separately
PROKOFIEFF, SERGE (1891-1953)	Music For Children Op. 65	L BH K GS I	Music for Children, Op. 65 (Summer Day Suite)
	1. Morning		
	2. Promenade	L MMC W	Published Separately Meet Modern Music, Pt. I Modern Russian Piano Music
	3. Fairy Tale	L MMC	Published Separately Meet Modern Music, Pt. I
	4. Tarantella	L Su	Published Separately Contemporary Piano Literature, Bk. 6 (Clark)
	5. Regrets	L	Published Separately
	6. Waltz	L L Su	Published Separately Children's Piano Pieces by Soviet Composers Contemporary Piano Literature, Bk. 5 (Clark)
	7. Parade of the Grasshopper	Su	Contemporary Piano Literature, Bk. 5 (Clark)
	8. Rain and the Rainbow	Su	Contemporary Piano Literature, Bk. 4 (Clark)
	9. Tag		
	10. March	L W L Su Su	Published Separately Modern Russian Piano Music Children's Piano Solos by Soviet Composers Contemporary Piano Literature, Bk. 4 (Clark) Musical Finds from the 20th Century (Podolsky)
	11. Evening	L BH Su	Published Separately From Ancient to Modern (Rowley) Contemporary Piano Literature, Bk. 6 (Clark)

Composer	Title	Publisher	Volume or Collection
PROKOFIEFF, SERGE (cont.)	12. Moonlit Meadows	Su	Contemporary Piano Literature, Bk. 6 (Clark)
		Su	Musical Finds from the 20th Century (Podolsky)
RAKOFF, NICOLAS (1908-)	Valse	W	Modern Russian Piano Music
RATHAUS, KAROL (1895-1954)	Cross Talk	CF	Published Separately

REBIKOV, VLADIMIR (1866-1920)	Piano Album, No. I
	  1. Little Story
	  2. A Letter
	  3. Berceuse
		Sch	Piano Album, No. I (Rowley)

	4. Country Fair	Su	Musical Finds from the 20th Century (Podolsky)

	5. Chinese Meditation
	  6. Chanson triste
	  7. Valse melancolique
	  8. Reverie
	  9. Mazurka
	10. Tender Reproach
	11. Turkish Dance
	12. In pensive mood
	13. In a mist
	14. Elegie
	15. Dance orientale
	16. Dance caractéres-
	     tique		

	Piano Album, No. II
	  1. In the Forest
	  2. Grotesque Dancer
	  6. Hope
		Sch	Piano Album, No. II (Rowley)

	8. Russian Doll (Kukla)	Su	Musical Finds from the 20th Century (Podolsky)

	9. Lilies of the Valley
	10. Valse Minature
	11. Autumn Flowers
	12. O Tell Me Why?
	13. Movements Plastiques
	     I
	14. Movements Plas-
	     tiques II
	15. The Vast Abyss
	17. Moments d'allegresse
	18. Danse avec une
	     Cloche
	20. Pavane
	21. Pages d'un manuscrit
	     oublié I
	22. Pages d'un manuscrit
	     oublié II		

Composer	Title	Publisher	Volume or Collection

REBIKOV,
VLADIMIR
(cont.)
	Pictures for Children,
	Op. 37
	  1. A Little Girl Pleading With Her Mother
	  2. Preparing the Lesson
	  3. A Picture from the Ancient World
	  4. A Joyous Moment
	  5. Up On A Swing
	  6. Promenade of the Gnomes
	  7. A Sad Story With A Happy Ending
		I	Pictures for Children, Op. 37

	Silhouettes, Op. 31	GS I	Silhouettes, Op. 31
	Children Skating Strolling Musicians Playing Soldiers	WR Su	Rediscovered Classics, Bk. I (Henderson) Musical Finds from the 20th Century (Podolsky)
	Evening in the Meadow Little Girl Rocking Her Dolly Shepherd Playing On His Pipe (The Little Shepherd) The Lame Witch Lurking in the Forest	WR	Rediscovered Classics, Bk. 2 (Henderson)

	Three Pieces from "Silhouettes," Op. 31
	  Children Skating
	  Hurdy Gurdy (Strolling Musicians
	  Playing Soldiers
		MMC	Meet Modern Music, Pt. I

REGER, MAX
(1873-1916)
	Jugend-Album I
	  1. Hasche mich!
	  2. Uber Stock und Stein
	  3. Frülingsluft
	  4. Reigen
	  5. Ein Tänzchen
	  6. Frohsinn
	  7. Das Tote Vöglein
		Sch	Jugend Album I

RHENE-BATON (1879-1940)	Musette	E E	Album Rose Published Separately
	Petit Choral		
ROBB, J. D. (1892-)	Horseback Over the Sagebrush Plain, (From "Pictures of New Mexico")	AMP	Published Separately

Composer	Title	Publisher	Volume or Collection
ROZSA, MIKLOS (1907-)	Musette, From "Kaleidoscope," Op. 19	AMP	Published Separately
RUBINSTEIN, BERYL (1898-1953)	Homeward Bound	CF	A Day In The Country
	The Brook		
	Musical Fancies, Series II 1. The Shepherd Boy 2. Minuet à la Reine 3. The Procession 4. Siciliana 5. The Little Match Girl	CF	Published Separately
SAMINSKY, LAZARE (1882-)	Firebell, Op. 45, No. 2	CF	Published Separately
	Parade, Op. 45, No. 4		
	Shadows, Op. 45, No. 3		
SCHULMAN, ALAN (1915-)	Cradle Song	Co	Published Separately
	Dripping Faucet	Co	
	March	Co	
SCHULTHESS, WALTER (1894-)	Glockenspiel	Sch	The New Piano Book, Vol. I
SCOTT, CYRIL (1879-)	A Little Dancer From Spain	Sch Sch	Miniatures Published Separately
	March of the Tin Soldiers, from "My Young Friends"	Su	Contemporary Piano Literature, Bk. 3 (Clark)
	Solitude, from "Young Hearts"	Sch	The New Piano Book, Vol. I
	Sunday Morn		
	The Zoo 1. The Elephant 2. The Squirrel 3. The Bear 4. The Monkey 5. The Snake 6. The Giraffe 7. The Tortoise 8. The Rhinoceros	Sch	The Zoo
SHULGIN, LEO	Children's Pieces 1. On the Steppes 2. On A Bicycle 3. In The Evening 4. Story 5. Cradle Song 6. Pioneer Meeting 7. Grandmother's Story 8. Turkmenian Song	L	Ten Children's Pieces

Composer	Title	Publisher	Volume or Collection
SHULGIN, LEO (cont.)	9. Meditation 10. To the Sound of the Accordian		
SIBELIUS, JAN (1865-1957)	Valsette	MMC	Meet Modern Music, Pt. I
SIEGMEISTER, ELIE (1909-)	From "The Children's Day" 1. Sunny Morning 2. Skipping Rope	L	The Children's Day
	Lonesome Song	TP	Published Separately
SLAVENSKI, JOSIP (1865-1930)	Albanian Song	Sch	The New Piano Book, Vol. I
STARER, ROBERT (1924-)	Bugle, Drum and Fife	TP	Published Separately
	The Telegraph	TP	Published Separately
STRAVINSKY, IGOR (1882-)	From "The Five Fingers" Allegro Heavily (Pesante)	O Sch MMC	The Five Fingers The New Piano Book, Vol. I Meet Modern Music, Pt. II
TANSMAN, ALEXANDRE (1897-)	From "Children At Play" 2. Two Voices 3. Elegy 4. Meditation	L Su	Children at Play Contemporary Piano Literature, Bk. 4 (Clark)
	5. Game 6. Barcarolle 7. Song 8. Lullaby 9. Toccata 10. Poem 11. Peasant Dance 12. Invention 13. South American Dance	Su Su Su	Bk. 4 Bk. 4 Bk. 4
	From "les Juenes au Piano" 1. Mireille 3. Les gros bouefs 5. La Mére Paule 7. L'escargot 8. Le chant du grillon 9. Le petit cheval au trot 10. La carpe dans l'etang 11. Les grenouilles 12. Dodo, Mireille	E	Mireille Et Les Animaux, Vol. I
	From "les Juenes au Piano" 2. Opéra 4. Quatier du Temple 5. Etoile	E	L'Autobus Imaginaire, Vol. III

Composer	Title	Publisher	Volume or Collection
TANSMAN, ALEXANDRE (cont.)	From "Ten Diversions for the Young Pianist" 1. Spanish Mood 2. Dreams 3. Merry-Go-Round 4. Melancholy 5. Rainy Day 6. Speeding Along 7. Calm 8. Prayer 9. Mischief	AMP	Ten Diversions for the Young Pianist
	Lullaby (From Children At Play)	L	Published Separately
	Piano Miniatures 1. Minuet 2. Caprice 3. Bourrée 4. Spleen	L	Piano Miniatures
	Pour les Enfants - Set I 1. Old Song 2. The Doll 3. The Bouncing Ball 4. The Dancing Bear 6. Russian Dance 9. Skating 11. Dream	E	Pour les Enfants
	Set II 5. Meditation 7. The Spinning Top 8. The Young Swing Pianist 9. The Dancing Lesson 10. Arabian Nights 11. Mickey and Minnie 12. Parade		Published Separately
	Set III 1. Awakening 2. The Warbler 3. Noel 4. Petite Rêverie 5. Tin Soldiers 6. Rest 7. Coquette 8. The Scooter 9. A Difficult Problem 10. The Old Beggar 11. The Music Box 12. Ping-Pong		Published Separately Published Separately Published Separately Publisned Separately Published Separately
	Set IV 1. An Old Tale 2. Rocking Horse 3. A Serious Moment 5. In A Venetian Gondola		Published Separately

Composer	Title	Publisher	Volume or Collection
TANSMAN, ALEXANDRE (cont.)	6. Blues Record 7. Valse Lento 9. Berceuse		Published Separately
	From "Recreations" Dream Etude Valse Walk	Su	Recreations
TCHÉREPNINE, ALEXANDRE (1899-)	Happy Stowaway	Su	Contemporary Piano Literature, Bk. 6 (Clark)
	Les Cloches tristes	D	Pour petits et grands - Set I
	Merry-Go-Round	Su	Contemporary Piano Literature, Bk. 4 (Clark)
	Mic and Mac	Su	Contemporary Piano Literature, Bk. 6
	Waltz	Su	Contemporary Piano Literature, Bk. 4
THOMPSON, RANDALL (1899-)	Little Prelude	CF	Masters of Our Day; 18 Solos in the Contemporary Idiom
	Song After Sundown		
THOMSON, VIRGIL (1896-)	A Day Dream	CF	Masters of Our Day; 18 Solos in the Contemporary Idiom
		CF	Published Separately
	Eccentric Dance	CF	Published Separately
TOCH, ERNST (1887-)	From "Echoes of A Small Town" 1. Little Kitten 2. Now I Lay Me Down To Sleep 6. Single File 13. Autumn Is Coming	AMP	Echoes of A Small Town, Op. 49
	Gray Skies, Op. 40, No. 13	Sch	The New Piano Book, Vol. I
	Sunbeams, Op. 20, No. 14		
VILLA-LOBOS, HEITOR (1887-1960)	Francette et Piá 1. Piá Came to France 2. Piá Saw Francette 3. Piá Spoke to Francette 4. Piá and Francette Play Together 5. Francette Is Sorry	E	Published Separately
	Petizada 1. My Right Hand Has A Rose 2. My Mother Used To Lullaby Me Like This	PI	Published Separately

Composer	Title	Publisher	Volume or Collection
VILLA-LOBOS, HEITOR (cont.)	3. The Poor, Little Country Girl 4. The Little White Dress 5. Sacy 6. The Story of Caprihina		
	The Toy Wheel 3. The Three Little Caballeros 4. One, Two Angolinhas	PI	Published Separately
WAXMAN, FRANZ (1906-)	From "The Charm Bracelet" 1. Two Little Shoes 2. The Four Leaf Clover	L	The Charm Bracelet Published Separately

SECTION III

INTERMEDIATE

GRADES V AND VI

MUSIC OF THE SIXTEENTH, SEVENTEENTH
AND EIGHTEENTH CENTURIES

Composer	Title	Publisher	Volume or Collection
AGINCOURT, F. de (1684-1757)	L'Etourdie	BH	Airs and Dances, Bk. II (Dorolle)
ANGLÉS, R. (1730-1816)	Sonata in F Major	Su	Portuguese and Spanish Keyboard Music
ARNE, T. (1710-1778)	Gigue (From Sonata VI in G Minor)	SG	Classics of the 17th and 18th Centuries
		CF	Classic Sonatas (Podolsky)
		A	Beringer's School of Easy Classics; Old English and French Masters
		B	Hours with the Masters, Bk. III
		PP	Hundred Best Short Classics, Bk. I
	Minuet with Variations	A	Beringer's School of Easy Classics: Old English and French Masters
		SG	Classics of the 17th and 18th Centuries
		B	Hours with the Masters, Bk. 4
		PP	Hundred Best Short Classics, Bk. I
	Sonata in B-flat	BH	Airs and Dances, Bk. I (Dorolle)
	Sonata in G Minor Affetuoso Gigue	CF	Classic Sonatas (Podolsky)
BACH, C. P. E. (1714-1788)	Alla Polacca, in A Minor	Sch	Die Söhne Bach
	Alla Polacca, in G	U	Clavierstücke—C.P.E. Bach
	Allegretto (From Sonata in F)	B	Hours with the Masters, Bk. II
	Andante in D	U	Old Masters for Young Pianists, Bk. 1 (Kuranda)
		U	Grosse meister für Kleine Hände, Bk. 1 (Kuranda)
	Fantasia	U	Clavierstücke--C. P. E. Bach
	Gigue in E Minor	He	Little Treasury of Classics, Bk. IV
	La Philippine	H	The Sons of Bach
	Larghetto from Sonata in G	K	Bach and His Contemporaries
	L'Auguste	U	Clavierstücke--C. P. E. Bach
	Les Languers Tendres	U	Clavierstücke--C. P. E. Bach
	Minuet in E	C	Eighteenth Century Music, Vol. II
	Presto in B-flat	Su	The Second Bach Book (Jonas)
		C	Eighteenth Century Music, Vol. II

Composer	Title	Publisher	Volume or Collection
BACH, C. P. E. (cont.)	Rondo in E-flat	P Su	Sonatas and Pieces The Second Back Book (Jonas)
	Sarabande	U	Clavierstücke—C.P.E. Bach
	Solfeggio in A	U	Clavierstücke—C. P. E. Bach

	Sonata I in C
	  Allegro tranquillamente
	  Andante
	  Tempo di Minuetto
		Sch	Six Sonatas by C. P. E. Bach, Vol. I

	Sonata in G
	  Allegretto
	  Andantino
	  Allegro
		Su	The Second Bach Book (Jonas)

BACH, J. C. (1735-1782)	Allegretto
	  (From Sonata Op. 5,
	  No. 1)
		EV	New Recital Repertoire (Mirovitch)

	Minuet (From Sonata in D, Op. 5, No. 2)	H	The Sons of Bach
	Tempo di Minuetto (From Sonata, Op. 5, No. 1)	EV	New Recital Repertoire (Mirovitch)
BACH, J. S. (1685-1750)	Allemande in A Minor	BMC CF	Bach for Early Grades, Bk. II Road to Piano Artistry, Vol. IV (Scionti)

	Aria für Klavier, in G
	  Major
		Sch
		K
			Little Bach Book (No. 13)
			Little Notebook of Anna Magdalena Bach
			  (pg. 77)

	Chorale, "O, Ewigkeit du Donnerwort"		(pg. 121)
	Choral "Wer nurden lieben Gott lässt walten"		(pg. 55)
	Entrée in F	Sch	Little Bach Book (No. 2)
	Fughetta in C Minor	K	Short Preludes and Fugues (pg. 22)
	Fugue in C	 GS GS Sch	(pg. 24) Eighteen Little Preludes and Fugues (No. 15) Short Preludes and Fugues (pg. 22) Little Bach Book (No. 16)

	Gavotte in D
	  (Gavotte II from
	  English Suite VI in
	  D Minor)
		K
		P
		GS
		CF
		GS
		GS
		CF
			English Suites
			English Suites, Vol. II
			English Suites
			Bach First Lessons, Bk. II (Carroll)
			First Lessons in Bach, Bk. II (Carroll)
			Bach Album (Heinze)

	Gavotte in G
	  (From French Suite V
	  in G)
		K
		P
		GS
			French Suites

Composer	Title	Publisher	Volume or Collection
BACH, J. S. (cont.)		ECS	Bach Verklärt
		CF	Bach First Lessons, Bk. II (Carroll)
		GS	First Lessons in Bach, Bk. II (Carroll)
		BMC	Bach for Early Grades, Bk. III
		GS	Bach Album (Heinze) (pg. 4)
		CF	
		B	Hours with the Masters, Bk. IV
		Su	Bach Collection, Berlinger/Jonas
	Gavottes in G Minor (From English Suite III)	K	English Suites
		P	
		GS	
		ECS	Bach Verklärt
		GS	Master Series for the Young
		GS	Bach Album (Heinze)
		CF	
		CF	Road to Piano Artistry, Vol. VI (Scionti)
		Su	Bach Collection (Berlinger/Jonas)
		MM	Your Bach Book (Maier)
	Gigue in C Minor (From French Suite II)	K	French Suites
		P	
		GS	
		BMC	Bach for Early Grades, Bk. III
	Invention in A Minor	K	Two-Part Inventions (No. 13)
		P	
		GS	
		P	Invention und Sinfonien
		K	Bach's Little Notebook for Wilhelm Friedemann Bach (No. 37)
	Invention in C	K	Two-Part Inventions (No. 1)
		P	
		GS	
		P	Inventionen und Sinfonien
		ECS	Bach Verklärt
		P	Sonatinen Album, Vol. II
		CF	Road to Piano Artistry, Vol. VII (Scionti)
		K	Bach's Little Notebook for Wilhelm Friedemann Bach (No. 32)
	Invention in D Minor	K	Two-Part Inventions (No. 4)
		P	
		GS	
		P	Inventionen und Sinfonien
		K	Bach's Little Notebook for Wilhelm Friedemann Bach (No. 33)
		MM	Your Bach Book
		B	Hours With the Masters, Bk. IV
	Invention in E Minor	K	Two-Part Inventions (No. 7)
		P	
		GS	
		P	Inventionen und Sinfonien
		K	Bach's Little Notebook for Wilhelm Friedemann Bach (No. 34)

Composer	Title	Publisher	Volume or Collection
BACH, J. S. (cont.)	Invention in F	K	Two-Part Inventions (No. 8)
		P	
		GS	
		BMC	Bach for Early Grades, Bk. III
		PP	Hundred Best Short Classics, Bk. 3
		P	Inventionen und Sinfonien
		K	Bach's Little Notebook for Wilhelm Friedemann Bach (No. 35)
	Invention in F Minor	K	Two-Part Inventions
		P	
		GS	
		P	Inventionen und Sinfonien
		K	Bach's Little Notebook for Wilhelm Friedemann Bach (No. 42)
	Little Prelude in C (No. 1 of Six Little Preludes)	K	Short Preludes and Fugues (pg. 16)
		P	Short Preludes and Fugues (pg. 17)
		GS	Short Preludes and Fugues (pg. 14)
		GS	Eighteen Little Preludes and Fugues (No. 5) (Key of B-flat)
	(Key of B-flat)	WR	Rediscovered Classics, Bk. 4 (Henderson)
		GS	Master Series for the Young (pg. 25)
		ECS	Bach Verklärt
	Little Prelude in C Minor	K	Short Preludes and Fugues (pg. 17)
		GS	Short Preludes and Fugues (pg. 15)
		P	Short Preludes and Fugues (pg. 18)
		Sch	Little Bach Book (No. 12)
		GS	Master Series for the Young
		Su	Bach Collection (Berlinger/Jonas)
	Little Prelude in D Minor	K	Short Preludes and Fugues (pg. 9)
		GS	Short Preludes and Fugues (pg. 7)
		P	Short Preludes and Fugues (pg. 8)
		GS	Eighteen Little Preludes and Fugues (No. 2)
		BMC	Bach for Early Grades, Bk. II
		K	First Bach Book (No. 30)
		CF	Road to Piano Artistry, Vol. III (Scionti)
		Sch	Little Piano Book of Wilhelm Friedemann Bach (pg. 12)
		K	Bach's Little Notebook for Wilhelm Friedemann Bach (No. 4)
		ECS	Bach Verklärt (No. 27)
	Little Prelude in D Minor	K	Short Preludes and Fugues (pg. 12)
		GS	Eighteen Little Preludes and Fugues (No. 14)
		GS	Short Preludes and Fugues (pg. 8)
		P	Short Preludes and Fugues (pg. 10)
		Sch	Little Bach Book (No. 7)
	Little Prelude in D Minor	K	Short Preludes and Fugues (pg. 18)
		P	Short Preludes and Fugues (pg. 20)
		GS	Short Preludes and Fugues (pg. 16)
		ECS	Bach Verklärt (No. 28)

Composer	Title	Publisher	Volume or Collection
BACH, J. S. (cont.)	Little Prelude in E Minor	K	Short Preludes and Fugues (pg. 10)
		P	Short Preludes and Fugues (pg. 10)
		GS	Short Preludes and Fugues (pg. 8)
		GS	Eighteen Little Preludes and Fugues (No. 10)
	Little Prelude in F	K	Short Preludes and Fugues (pg. 11)
		P	Short Preludes and Fugues (pg. 11)
		GS	Short Preludes and Fugues (pg. 9)
		K	Bach's Little Notebook for Wilhelm Friedemann Bach (No. 8)
		WR	Rediscovered Classics, Bk. 2
		Su	Piano Literature of the 17th, 18th and 19th Centuries, Bk. 5a (Clark)
		K	First Bach Book (pg. 26)
		Sch	Little Piano Book of Wilhelm Friedemann Bach (No. 7)
	Little Prelude in G Minor	K	Short Preludes and Fugues (pg. 13)
		P	Short Preludes and Fugues (pg. 14)
		GS	Short Preludes and Fugues (pg. 11)
		K	Bach's Little Notebook for Wilhelm Friedemann Bach (No. 9)
		K	First Bach Book (No. 23)
		Sch	Little Piano Book of Wilhelm Friedemann Bach (No. 9)
	Marche in E-flat	K	Little Notebook of Anna Magdalena Bach (pg. 72)
		K	First Bach Book (No. 17)
		GS	First Lessons in Bach, Bk. I (Carroll)
		CF	Bach First Lessons, Bk. I (Carroll)
		GS	Master Series for the Young
	Menuet in C Minor	K	French Suites
		P	
		GS	
		BMC	Bach for Early Grades, Bk. III
	Polonaise in F	K	Little Notebook of Anna Magdalena Bach (pg. 51)
		P	Notenbuch der Anna Magdalena Bach (Sauer)
	Polonaise in G	K	Little Notebook of Anna Magdalena Bach (pg. 82)
		CF	Bach First Lessons, Bk. II
	Polonaise in G Minor	K	Little Notebook of Anna Magdalena Bach (pg. 66)
		P	Notenbuch der Anna Magdalena Bach (No. 14) (Sauer)
		CF	Bach First Lessons, Bk. II (Carroll) (No. 1)
		GS	First Lessons in Bach, Bk. II (Carroll) (No. 1)
		GS	Master Series for the Young (pg. 24)

Composer	Title	Publisher	Volume or Collection
BACH, J. S. (cont.)	Polonaise in G Minor	K	Little Notebook of Anna Magdalena Bach (pg. 62)
		P	Notenbuch der Anna Magdalena Bach (No. 12) (Sauer)
		CF	Bach First Lessons, Bk. II (Carroll) (No. 6)
		GS	First Lessons in Bach, Bk. II (Carroll) (No. 6)
BACH, W. F. (1710-1784)	Allegro in A	SG	Classics from the 17th and 18th Centuries (Tapper)
BENDA, F. (1709-1786)	Sonatina in D Minor	Sch	Simple Short Piano Pieces
		GS	Introduction to Piano Classics, Vol. II (Mirovitch)
	Sonatina in G	Sch	Simple Short Piano Pieces
		GS	Introduction to Piano Classics, Vol. II (Mirovitch)
BYRD, W. (1542 or '43- 1623)	Galiardo in A Minor	GS	Early Keyboard Music, Vol. I
	Pavanne (From "The Earl of Salisbury")	GS	Early Keyboard Music, Vol. I
		B	Hours with the Masters, Bk. III
		PP	Hundred Best Short Classics, Bk. II
	Preludium in C	GS	Early Keyboard Music, Vol. I
CASANOVAS, N. (1747-1794)	Sonata in F Major	Su	Portuguese and Spanish Keyboard Music
CHAMBONNIÈRES, J. C. de (1602-1670)	Sarabande in G	GS	Early Keyboard Music, Vol. I
CIMAROSA, D. (1749-1801)	Sonatas Nos. 2, 5, 9	E	Thirty-two Sonatas, Vol. I
	Sonatas, Nos. 13, 15, 16, 17	E	Thirty-two Sonatas, Vol. II
CORELLI, A. (1653-1713)	Gavotte in E (No. 10)	K	Corelli, 24 Pieces for the Piano, Vol. I
	Adagio (No. 2)		
	Adagio (No. 8)		
	Allegro (No. 11)		
	Largo (No. 9)		
	Präeludium (No. 4)		
	Präeludium (No. 7)		
	Sarabande in D Minor (No. 5)		
	Sarabande in B-flat (No. 6)		
COUPERIN, F. (1668-1733)	La Commére	B	Hours with the Masters, Bk. V
	Le Moucheron	B	Hours with the Masters, Bk. III
	Les Moissonneurs	GS	Early Keyboard Music, Vol. II

Composer	Title	Publisher	Volume or Collection
COUPERIN, F. (cont.)		BH	Airs and Dances, Bk. I (Dorolle)
		A	Beringer's School of Easy Classics: Old English and French Masters
DANDRIEU, A. (1684-1740)	Le Timpanon	BH	Airs and Dances, Bk. I (Dorolle)
DAQUIN, C. (1694-1772)	La Melodieuse	BH	Airs and Dances, Bk. II
DITTERSDORF, K. (1739-1799)	Allegro in E	Sch	Simple Short Piano Pieces (Kreutz) (No. 9)
DUSSEK, J. L. (1760-1812)	Larghetto quasi andante	EV	New Recital Repertoire (Mirovitch)
	Sonatina, Op. 20, No. 1 Allegro non tanto Rondo	GS	Album of Sonatinas
	Sonatina, Op. 20, No. 2 Allegretto quasi andante Rondo		
	Sonatina, Op. 20, No. 3 Allegro quasi presto Rondo	GS	Selected Sonatinas, Bk. II
FISCHER, J. K. F. (1650-1746)	Gigue in G	Sch	Notebook of Johann Kaspar Ferd. Fischer
	Fughette in D		
	Fugue in A Minor	K	A Little Book of Fugues (No. 3)
	Fugue in A Minor		(No. 4)
	Fugue in F		(No. 14)
	Fugue in G Minor		(No. 9)
FLEISCHER, F. G. (1722-1806)	Minuetto in F	Sch	Menuetten fürs Clavier
	Minuetto I in G		
	Minuetto II in G		
FRESCOBALDI, G. (1583-1644)	Corrente	B	Hours with the Masters, Bk. III
	Gagliarda in G Minor	GS	Early Keyboard Music, Bk. I
GALLÉS, J. (1781-1836)	Sonata in C Minor	Su	Portuguese and Spanish Keyboard Music
GALUPPI, B. (1706-1785)	Allegro	GS	Early Classics for the Piano (Mirovitch)
	Minuet in E-flat	EHM	Discoveries for Piano (Mirovitch)
	Presto		
	Sonata	TP	Eighteenth Century Italian Keyboard Music

Composer	Title	Publisher	Volume or Collection
GRAUN, C. H. (1701-1759)	Andante in F	U	Grosse Meister für Kleine Hände, Bk. 2 (Kuranda)
		U	Old Masters for Young Pianists (Kuranda) Bk. 2
GRAUPNER, C. (1683-1760)	Air en Gavotte in D	P	Contemporaries of Telemann (No. 9)
GRÉTRY, A. E. (1741-1813)	Gigue in E-flat	A	Beringer's School of Easy Classics: Old English and French Masters
GRIECO (1680- ?)	Aria di Ballo	HC	Clavecinistes Italiens (No. 6)
GROSSE, M. C. (2nd half of 18th century)	Minuetto I in A	Sch	Minuetten fürs Clavier
	Minuetto II in A		
HANDEL, G. F. (1685-1759)	Air in D Minor (From Suite X)	P	Handel Suites, Vol. I
		K	Handel Suites, Vol. II
	Air in G Minor	Sch	Pieces for Harpsichord, Vol. I (No. 25)
	Allegro in G Major	PP	Hundred Best Short Classics, Bk. V
	A tempo guisto	Sch	Pieces for Harpsichord, Vol. I (No. 27)
	Chaconne in G (From Chaconne with 62 Variations)	GS	Master Series for the Young
	Chaconne in G Minor	Sch	Pieces for Harpsichord, Vol. I (No. 5)
	Courante in F Major	PP	Hundred Best Short Classics, Bk. II
		GS	Handel: 12 Easy Pieces
		B	Hours with the Masters, Bk. II
		H	Easiest Original Pieces
		BH	Airs and Dances, Bk. II (Dorolle)
		Su	Piano Literature of the 17th, 18th and 19th Centuries, Bk. 5a (Clark)
	Fuga in G	Sch	Aylesford Pieces (No. 5)
		Sch	Pieces for Harpsichord, Vol. II (No. 50)
	Gavotte in G	Sch	Aylesford Pieces (No. 3)
		Sch	Pieces for Harpsichord, Vol. I (No. 6)
	Gavotte in C	H	Easiest Original Pieces
		GS	Handel: 12 Easy Pieces
	Gavotte in G Minor	Sch	Pieces for Harpsichord, Vol. I (No. 24)
	Little Fugue in C (No. 1)	GS	Master Series for the Young
		K	Bach and His Contemporaries
	Little Sonata in C	U	Old Masters for Young Pianists, Bk. 1 (Kuranda)
		U	Grosse Meister für Kleine Hände, Bk. 1 (Kuranda)
	Menuet in A Minor	Sch	Pieces for Harpsichord, Vol. II (No. 67)

Composer	Title	Publisher	Volume or Collection
HANDEL, G. F. (cont.)	Menuet in D	Sch	Vol. I (No. 30)
	Menuet in F		(No. 9)
	Menuet in G Minor		(No. 65)
	Menuetto in B-flat (From Suite in B-flat)	K	Handel Suites, Vol. II
	Minuet in F	Sch	Pieces for Harpsichord, Vol. II (No. 60)
		Sch	Aylesford Pieces (No. 14)
	Minuet in F Minor	Sch	Pieces for Harpsichord, Vol. II (No. 59)
		Sch	Aylesford Pieces (No. 15)
	Minuet in G Minor	Sch	Pieces for Harpsichord, Vol. I (No. 29)
	Prelude in G	GS	Master Series for the Young
		He	A Treasury of Easy Classics (Abrams)
	Sarabande in D Minor (From Suite XI)	P	Handel Suites, Vol. II
		K	Handel Suites, Vol. II
		GS	Handel: 12 Easy Pieces
		U	Old Masters for Young Pianists, Bk. 1 (Kuranda)
		U	Grosse meister für Kleine Hände, Bk. 1 (Kuranda)
		H	Easiest Original Pieces
		CF	Road to Piano Artistry, Vol. VI (Scionti)
		GS	Master Series for the Young
	Sarabande in D Minor (From Suite XV)	P	Suites, Vol. II
		Su	Piano Literature of the 17th, 18th and 19th Centuries, Bk. 5a (Clark)
		P	Sonatinen Album, Vol. II
	Sarabande in E Minor (From Suite IV)	P	Handel Suites, Vol. I
		K	
	Sarabande in E	Sch	Pieces for Harpsichord, Vol. II (No. 16)
	Sarabande in F		(No. 23)
	Sarabande in G Minor (From Suite VII)	P	Suites, Vol. I
		K	
	Toccata in G Minor	Sch	Pieces for Harpsichord, Vol. I (No. 26)
		Sch	Aylesford Pieces (No. 4)
HÄSSLER, J. W. (1747-1822)	Menuetto	EHM	Discoveries for Piano (Mirovitch)
	Minuetto I in A	Sch	Menuetten fürs Clavier
	Minuetto II in A		
	Scherzo in A	GS	Early Classics for the Piano (Mirovitch)
	Scherzo in D		
	Scherzo in E Minor	EHM	Discoveries for Piano (Mirovitch)
HAYDN, J. (1732-1809)	Andante in E Minor (Sonata from State Library in Berlin)	WR	Rediscovered Classics, Bk. 4 (Henderson)

Composer	Title	Publisher	Volume or Collection
HAYDN, J. (cont.)	Finale: Allegro (From Sonata in C, No. 5)	P	Haydn Sonatas, Vol. I
		K	Haydn Sonatas, Vol. I (No. 5)
		GS	Haydn Sonatas, Vol. I
		U	Haydn Sonatas, Vol. I (No. 2)
		GS	Master Series for the Young
	Finale: Presto (From unfinished Sonata in A)	WR	Rediscovered Classics, Bk. 3 (Henderson)
	Finale: Presto (From Sonata in A, No. 33)	P	Haydn Sonatas, Vol. III
	La Roxalane (Air Varie)	K	Haydn: 8 Various Compositions for Piano
		A	Beringer's School of Easy Classics: Haydn
		GS	Master Series for the Young
		EV	New Recital Repertoire (Mirovitch)
	Menuetto (From Sonata in A)	P	Haydn Sonatas, Vol. III (No. 33)
	Menuetto (From Sonata in B-flat)	P	Haydn Sonatas, Vol. II (No. 22)
		H	Easiest Original Pieces
	Menuetto: Moderato (From Sonata in C-sharp minor)	P	Haydn Sonatas, Vol. I (No. 6)
		K	Haydn Sonatas, Vol. Ia (No. 6)
		GS	Haydn Sonatas, Vol. I (No. 6)
		U	Haydn Sonatas, Vol. III (No. 20)
	Menuetto (From Sonata in E)	P	Haydn Sonatas, Vol. II (No. 18)
		K	Haydn Sonatas, Vol. Ib (No. 17)
		GS	Haydn Sonatas, Vol. II (No. 17)
		GS	Master Series for the Young
		U	Haydn Sonatas, Vol. I (No. 4)
	Scherzando (From Sonata in C-sharp minor)	P	Haydn Sonatas, Vol. I (No. 6)
		K	Haydn Sonatas, Vol. Ia (No. 6)
		GS	Haydn Sonatas, Vol. I (No. 6)
		U	Haydn Sonatas, Vol. III (No. 20)

	Sonatina in C
	  Allegro
	  Andante
	  Menuet
		P	Six Little Divertimenti (No. 1)

	Sonatina in C
	  Allegro
	  Andante
	  Menuet
		P	Six Little Divertimenti (No. 2)

	Sonatina in C
	  Moderato
	  Menuet
	  Finale
		AMP
		P
			Haydn: Six Sonatinas (No. 5)
			Haydn Sonatas, Vol. IV (No. 43)

	Sonatina in D
	  Allegro
	  Menuetto
		AMP
		H
		P
			Haydn: Six Sonatinas (No. 1)
			Easiest Original Pieces
			Six Little Divertimenti (No. 3)

	Sonatina in F
	  Allegro
	  Scherzo
		AMP	Haydn: Six Sonatinas (No. 4)
			Six Little Divertimenti (No. 6)

Composer	Title	Publisher	Volume or Collection
HAYDN, J. (cont.)	Sonatina in G	AMP	Haydn: Six Sonatinas (No. 6)
	Presto	P	Haydn Sonatas, Vol. I (No. 11)
	Andante		
	Menuet		
HILLER, J. A. (1728-1804)	Minuet in A	GS	Introduction to Piano Classics, Vol. II (Mirovitch)
KIRNBERGER, J. P. (1721-1783)	Aria and Variation	Su	Kirnberger Collection (Jonas)
	Bourée, A Major	Su	Kirnberger Collection (Jonas)
	Gavotte in D	Sch	Clavierstücke für Anfänger
		Su	Kirnberger Collection (Jonas)
	Gavotte in D Minor	K	Old Masters of the 16th, 17th and 18th Centuries
	Four Small Pieces	K	Old Masters of the 16th, 17th and 18th Centuries (pg. 34)
	1. Polonaise in G Minor	Su	Kirnberger Collection (Jonas)
	2. Menuet in D		
	3. La Lutine		
	4. La Galliard		
	Passepied in E	Su	Kirnberger Collection (Jonas)
		GS	Introduction to Piano Classics, Vol. I
	Polonaise in D	GS	Introduction to Piano Classics, Vol. I
	Presto	Su	Kirnberger Collection (Jonas)
	Rondo in E Major		
KREBS, J. (1713-1780)	Allegro in G	Sch	Simple Short Piano Pieces
		GS	Introduction to Piano Classics, Vol. II (Mirovitch)
	Bourrée in E-flat	U	Grosse Meister für kleine Hände
	Bourrée in G Minor	P	Contemporaries of Telemann
	Toccata in E-flat (Allegro)	GS	Introduction to Piano Classics, Vol. II (Mirovitch)
		Sch	Simple Short Piano Pieces
KUHNAU, J. (1660-1722)	Gavotte in D	U	Grosse Meister für Kleine Hände, Bk. 2
	Praeludium in E Minor (From Suite III)	GS	Early Keyboard Music, Bk. I
		GS	Introduction to Piano Classics, Vol. II (Mirovitch)
	Sarabande (From Suite III)	GS	Early Keyboard Music, Bk. I
LEO, LEONARDO (1694-1744)	Toccata	GS	Early Classics for the Piano (Mirovitch)
LOEILLET, J. (1653-1728)	Sarabande in A	H	Contemporaries of Purcell
MARPURG, F. W. (1718-1795)	Menuet in G	K	Old Masters of the 16th, 17th and 18th Centuries

Composer	Title	Publisher	Volume or Collection
MARPURG, F. W. (cont.)	Prélude in G	BH	Airs and Dances, Bk. II
MARTINI, G. (1706-1784)	Gavotte in F Major	K	Old Masters of the 16th, 17th and 18th Centuries
		PP	Hundred Best Classics, Bk. III
MATTHESON, J. (1681-1764)	Fantasy, C. Minor	K	Bach and His Contemporaries, Bk. 2
	Menuett (From Suite V in C Minor)	GS	Early Keyboard Music, Bk. II
MONN (MANN), J. C. (1726-1782)	Siciliana	U	Grosse Meister für Kleine Hände, Bk. 2
MOURET, J. J. (1682-1735)	Bourrée in E	A	Beringer's School of Easy Classics: Old English and French Masters
MOZART, W. A. (1756-1791)	Adagio in A	Sch I MMC H He GS	Six Viennese Sonatinas (No. 2)
	Adagio in C	Sch I MMC He GS H	Six Viennese Sonatinas (No. 1)
	Allegro Grazioso	GS	Master Series for the Young
	Allegro in C (K 6)	Sch	Notebook for Nannerl Mozart
	Andante in D	Sch H I MMC He GS	Six Viennese Sonatinas (No. 3)
	Andante in G (K 545)	K P GS	Mozart Sonatas / Mozart Sonatas, Vol. II / Master Series for the Young
	Four Unknown Miniatures 1. Theme for Variations (K 383d) 2. Marche Funébre (K 453a) 3. Tempo di Minuetto (K 526a) 4. Rondo (K 590c)	Ox	Four Unknown Miniatures (Werner)
	Menuetto in A	Sch H	Six Viennese Sonatinas (No. 2)

Composer	Title	Publisher	Volume or Collection
MOZART, W. A. (cont.)		I MMC He GS	
	Menuetten I and II (K 282)	K P B K	Mozart Sonatas Mozart Sonatas, Vol. I Hours with the Masters, Bk. IV Easy Compositions by Mozart and Beethoven
	Menuetto in C	Sch MMC I He H GS CF	Six Viennese Sonatinas (No. 6) Road to Piano Artistry, Vol. VIII (Scionti)
	Menuetto in D	Sch MMC H He I GS K	Six Viennese Sonatinas (No. 3) Easy Composition by Mozart and Beethoven
	Mio Caro Adone (K 180)	K	Easy Compositions by Mozart and Beethoven
	Polonaise in F (From Viennese Sonatina in F)	WR	Rediscovered Classics, Bk. I (Henderson)
	Rondo in C (K 545)	K P GS B P	Mozart Sonatas Mozart Sonatas, Vol. II Master Series for the Young Hours with the Masters, Bk. II Sonaten, Album, Vol. I
	Rondo in D	Sch	The Young Mozart
	Sonata in C (K 545) Allegro Andante Rondo	K P P P R	Mozart Sonatas Mozart Sonatas, Vol. II Sonaten Album, Vol. I Sonatinen Album, Vol. I Haydn-Mozart, Easy Compositions
	Sonatina in F	Sch MMC H He GS I	Six Viennese Sonatinas (No. 5)
MUFFAT, G. T. (1690-1770)	Capriccio desperato	Sch	Partiten und Stücke
	Gavotte (From Partita in C Minor)		

Composer	Title	Publisher	Volume or Collection
MUFFAT, G. T. (cont.)	Harlequin		
	Menuet (From Partita in C)		
	Menuet (From Partita in C Minor)		
	Menuet in B-flat	GS	Introduction to Piano Classics, Vol. III (Mirovitch)
	Menuet in D	P	Contemporaries of Telemann
	Prelude, (From Partita in C)	Sch	Partiten und Stücke
	Rigaudon in C	U	Grosse Meister für Kleine Hände
	Sarabande, (From Partita in C Minor)	Sch	Partiten und Stücke
	Siciliana	Sch	Partiten und Stücke
MURCHHAUSER, F. (1663-1738)	Fugue in C Major, No. 2	K	A Little Book of Fugues
NEEFE, C. G. (1748-1798)	Minuetto in F	Sch	Menuetten furs Clavier (Kreutz)
NICHELMANN, C. (1717-1762)	Sarabande in C Minor	K	Old Masters of the 16th, 17th and 18th Centuries
PESCETTI, G. B. (1704-1766)	Allegretto in C	HC	Clavecinistes Italiens (No. 4)
PURCELL, H. (1658-1695)	Air in G Minor	H	Contemporaries of Purcell
	Air On A Ground Bass	WR	Rediscovered Classics, Bk. 4 (Henderson)
	Hornpipe in E Minor	PP / He	Frederick Moore Collection / A Little Treasury of Classics, Bk. IV (Lambert)
	Intrada and March, (From Suite in C, No. 5)	GS / GS	Purcell: Keyboard Suites / Early Keyboard Music, Vol. 1
	Minuet, (From Suite in F, No. 8)	GS / GS	Purcell: Keyboard Suites / Early Keyboard Music, Vol. 1
	Riggadoon, (From Suite in C, No. 5)	GS / GS	Purcell: Keyboard Suites / Early Keyboard Music, Vol. I
	Suite in G, No. 1 Prelude Almand Courante Minuet	GS / GS	Purcell: Keyboard Suites / Early Keyboard Music, Vol. I
RAMEAU, J. P. (1683-1764)	La Joyeuse	B	Hours with the Masters, Bk. IV
	Les Tendres Plaintes	BH	Airs and Dances, Bk. II (Dorolle)

Composer	Title	Publisher	Volume or Collection
RAMEAU, J. P. (cont.)		GS	Early Keyboard Music, Bk. II
		A	Beringer's School of Easy Classics: Old English and French Masters
	Rigaudon in E Minor	GS	Early Keyboard Music, Bk. II
		B	Hours with the Masters, Bk. II
		K	Old Masters of the 16th, 17th and 18th Centuries
	Tambourin	A	Beringer's School of Easy Classics: Old English and French Masters
		GS	Early Keyboard Music, Bk. II
		PP	Hundred Best Short Classics, Bk. III (Lambert)
		GS	Published Separately
		JF	Published Separately
		He	A Little Treasury of Classics, Bk. 2
REICHARDT, J. F. (1752-1814)	Aria in G Minor	EV	New Recital Repertoire (Mirovitch)
	Scherzando in D	GS	Introduction to Piano Classics, Vol. II (Mirovitch)
RODRIGUES, F. (1759-1814)	Rondo in B-flat Major	Su	Portuguese and Spanish Keyboard Music
ROSSI, M. A. de (1720-1794)	Allegro sostenuto	HC	Clavecinistes Italiens (No. 1)
ROSSI, M. (? -1660)	Andantino	K	Old Italian Masters
RUTINI, G. M. (1730-1797)	Menuetto in C	TP	Eighteenth Century Italian Keyboard Music
		HC	Clavecinistes Italiens (No. 7)
SACCHINI, A. (1734-1786)	Sonata per il Cembalo	TP	Eighteenth Century Italian Keyboard Music
SANDER, F. S. (1760-1796)	Sonatina in G Allegretto Larghetto Allegro ma non troppo	Sch	Clavier Sonatinen (Kreutz)
SANTELLI, A. (1720-1760)	Prelude	K	Old Italian Masters
SARTI, G. (1729-1802)	Allegro piuttosto moderato	HC	Clavecinistes Italiens
SCARLATTI, D. (1685-1757)	Air with Variations in A Minor	A	Beringer's School of Easy Classics: Scarlatti
	Allegro in D	He	A Treasury of Easy Classics (Abrams)

Composer	Title	Publisher	Volume or Collection
SCARLATTI, D. (cont.)	Allegretto in E Minor	A	Beringer's School of Easy Classics: Scarlatti
	Minuetto in B-flat	He	A Treasury of Easy Classics (Abrams)
	Siciliano in D Minor	PP	Hundred Best Short Classics, Bk. I
	Siciliano in F	A	Beringer's School of Easy Classics: Scarlatti (No. 3)
	Sonatas	M	Twelve Easy Scarlatti Sonatas (Mirovitch)
	1. D Minor (L 423)	Su	Piano Literature of the 17th, 18th and 19th Centuries, Bk. 5a (Clark)
	2. G (L 83)	Su	Piano Literature, Bk. 5a (Clark)
	3. G (L 79)	Su	Piano Literature of the 17th, 18th and 19th Centuries, Bk. 4a (Clark)
	4. G (L 84)	A	Beringer's School of Easy Classics: Scarlatti
	5. B-flat (L 97)		
	6. D Minor (L 58)	Su	Piano Literature of the 17th, 18th and 19th Centuries, Bk. 5a (Clark)
	Sonata, L 53	EHM	Discoveries for Piano (Mirovitch)
	Sonata, L 75		
SCHILLING, F. W. (2nd half of 18th Century)	Sonatina in B-flat Andantino Allegro	Sch	Clavier Sonatinen (Kreutz)
SEIXAS, C. (1704-1742)	Gigue in D Minor	Su	Portuguese and Spanish Keyboard Music
	Toccata in C Minor		
	Toccata in G Minor		
TELEMANN, G. P. (1681-1767)	Aria (From G Major Partita)	P	Contemporaries of Telemann
	Bourrée in A	P	Contemporaries of Telemann
	Fantasia in D, No. I	Sch EV	Telemann: Kleine Fantasien New Recital Repertoire (Mirovitch)
	Fantasia in F	Sch	Notebook for Wolfgang
	Gavotte (From Overture in A Minor)	P	Contemporaries of Telemann
	Presto in G	GS	Introduction to Piano Classics, Vol. II (Mirovitch)
	Rigaudon I, II	P	Contemporaries of Telemann
TÜRK, D. G. (Tuerk) (1750-1813)	Andantino in F	Sch	Simple Short Piano Pieces
WITTHAUER, J. G. (1750-1802)	Menuetto in F	Sch	Menuetten fürs Clavier
	Sonate in B-flat Poco moderato ed affetuoso	Sch	Clavier Sonatinen (Kreutz)

Composer	Title	Publisher	Volume or Collection
WITTHAUER, J. G. (cont.)	Larghetto Allegro scherzando		
WOLF, E. W. (1735-1792)	Sonatina in C Minor Larghetto Allegretto	Sch	Clavier Sonatinen (Kreutz)
WOLF, G. F. (1762-1814)	Sonatina in D Allegretto grazioso Menuetto con Trio Allegro scherzando	Sch	Clavier Sonatinen (Kreutz)
ZIPOLI, D. (1675-1726)	Aria in B Minor	K	Old Masters of the 16th, 17th and 18th Centuries
	Gavotta	HC	Clavecinistes Italiens
	Preludio in B Minor	K	Old Masters of the 16th, 17th and 18th Centuries

Composer	Title	Publisher	Volume or Collection
BEETHOVEN, L. van (1770-1827)	Adagio in F (From Un- finished Sonata in C)	WR	Rediscovered Classics, Bk. 2 (Henderson)
	Adieu to the Piano	GS	Published Separately
	Bagatelle in A, Op. 119, No. 4	K	Various Piano Pieces
		P	Various Pieces
		K	Easy Compositions by Mozart and Beethoven
		H	Easiest Original Pieces
		B	Hours With the Masters, Bk. 4
	Bagatelle in A, Op. 119, No. 10	K	Various Piano Pieces
		P	Various Pieces
		H	Easiest Original Pieces
	Bagatelle in A Minor, Op. 119, No. 9	K	Various Piano Pieces
		P	Various Pieces
		H	Easiest Original Pieces
	Bagatelle in D, Op. 119, No. 3	K	Various Piano Pieces
		P	Various Pieces
		H	Easiest Original Pieces
		CF	Road to Piano Artistry, Vol. V (Scionti)
		PP	Hundred Best Short Classics, Bk. II
		GS	Master Series for the Young
	Bagatelle in F, Op. 33, No. 3	K	Various Piano Pieces
		P	Various Pieces
		B	Hours with the Masters, Bk. II
		GS	Beethoven: Easy Compositions
	Ländler in D	K	Easy Compositions by Mozart and Beethoven
	Country Dance, No. 5	Su	Piano Literature of the 17th, 18th and 19th Centuries, Bk. 5b (Clark)
	Minuet in D	H	Easiest Original Pieces (No. 3)
	Six Easy Variations on a Swiss Song	K	Variations, Vol. II
		P	
		GS	
		K	Easy Compositions by Mozart and Beethoven
		GS	Master Series for the Young
		Su	Piano Literature of the 17th, 18th and 19th Centuries, Bk. 5b (Clark)
		A	Published Separately
	Sonata in G, Op. 49, No. 2 Allegro ma non troppo Tempo di Minuetto	K	Sonatas, Vol. II
		SS	
		P	Sonaten Album, Vol. I
		P	Sonatinen Album, Vol. I

Composer	Title	Publisher	Volume or Collection
BEETHOVEN, L. van (cont.)		GS	Album of Sonatinas
		GS	Thirty-two Sonatinas and Rondos
		CF	Road to Piano Artistry, Vol. VII (Scionti)
	Sonatina in C Allegro Adagio	K P	Beethoven Sonatinas
	Waltz in F	Sch	Kleine Tänze (Frey) (No. 12)
BORODIN. A. (1834-1887)	Au Convent	GS P GS	Published Separately Petite Suite Introduction to Piano Classics, Vol. II (Mirovitch)
	Reverie	P	Petite Suite
BRAHMS, J. (1833-1897)	Waltz in A-flat, Op. 39, No. 15	GS P K	Waltzes, Op. 39
	Waltz in D Minor, Op. 39, No. 9	GS P K H	Waltzes, Op. 39 Contemporaries of Schumann
	Waltz in G Sharp Minor, Op. 39, No. 3	GS P K	Waltzes, Op. 39
CHOPIN, F. (1810-1849)	Mazurka in B-flat, Op. 7, No. 1	GS K P PMP CF GS GS	Mazurkas Road to Piano Artistry, Vol. VIII (Scionti) Master Series for the Young Chopin Album
	Mazurka in F, Op. 68, No. 3	GS K P PMP GS	Mazurkas Master Series for the Young
	Prelude in B Minor, Op. 28, No. 6	GS K P PMP GS H PP He GS	Preludes, Op. 28 Master Series for the Young Easiest Original Pieces Hundred Best Short Classics, Bk. IV Little Treasury of Classics, Bk. IV Selected Piano Solos by Romantic Composers, Bk. II
	Prelude in E Minor, Op. 28, No. 4	GS K P PMP H	Preludes, Op. 28 Easiest Original Pieces

Composer	Title	Publisher	Volume or Collection
CHOPIN, F. (cont.)		PP	Hundred Best Short Classics, Bk. IV
		GS	Selected Piano Solos by Romantic Composers, Bk. II
CLEMENTI, M. (1752-1832)	Adagio in C (From Sonatina, Op. 39, No. 2)	WR	Rediscovered Classics, Bk. 4 (Henderson)
	Rondo in G (From Op. 36, No. 5)	GS	Clementi: Six Sonatinas, Op. 36
		P	
		P	Clementi Sonatinas, Op. 36, 37, 38
		P	Sonatinen Album, Vol. I
		GS	Album of Sonatinas
		GS	Published Separately
	Sonatina in B-flat, Op. 38, No. 2 Allegro Moderato Rondo	GS P P	Clementi Sonatinas Clementi Sonatinas, Op. 36, 37, 38 Sonatinen Album, Vol. II
	Sonatina in C, Op. 36, No. 3 Spiritoso Un poco adagio Allegro	GS P P P GS GS	Clementi: Six Sonatinas, Op. 36 Clementi Sonatinas, Op. 36, 37, 38 Sonatinen Album, Vol. I Thirty-two Sonatinas and Rondos Published Separately
	Sonatina in C, Op. 37 No. 3 Allegro Spiritoso Allegro	GS P	Clementi, 12 Sonatinas Clementi Sonatinas, Op. 36, 37, 38
	Sonatina, in D, Op. 37, No. 2 Allegro Assai Menuetto	P P	Sonatinen Album, Vol. II Clementi Sonatinas, Op. 36, 37, 38
	Sonatina in G, Op. 38, No. 1 Allegro Tempo di Minuetto	P P	Sonatinen Album, Vol. II Clementi Sonatinas, Op. 36, 37, 38
	Sonatina in E-flat, Op. 37, No. 1 Andantino Presto	GS P	Clementi Sonatinas Clementi Sonatinas, Op. 36, 37, 38
	Sonatina in F, Op. 36, No. 4 Con spirito Andante con espressione Rondo: Allegro vivace	GS P GS GS CF GS P	Clementi: Six Sonatinas, Op. 36 Album of Sonatinas Thirty-two Sonatinas and Rondos Road to Piano Artistry, Vol. V (Scionti) Published Separately Sonatinen Album, Vol. I
	Waltz in C	P	Sonatinen Vorstufe, Vol. II
	Waltz in E-flat	EV	New Recital Repertoire (Mirovitch)
	Waltz, No. 22	EHM	Discoveries for Piano (Mirovitch)

Composer	Title	Publisher	Volume or Collection
CRAMER, J. B. (1771-1858)	Variations on an Old English Air	WR	Rediscovered Classics, Bk. 3 (Henderson)
FIELD, J. (1782-1837)	Nocturne in B-flat	GS P GS	Field: Eighteen Nocturnes Field Nocturnes Published Separately
GADE, N. (1817-1890)	Album-Leaf (From Three Album-Leaves)	H	Contemporaries of Schumann
	Barcarolle, Op. 19, No. 5	CF	Road to Piano Artistry, Vol. V (Scionti)
	Elegie, Op. 19, No. 1	B	Hours with the Masters, Bk. III (Podolsky)
	Novelette, Op. 19	WR	Rediscovered Classics, Bk. 4 (Henderson)
GRIEG, E. (1843-1907)	Album Leaf, Op. 28, No. 2	GS P GS	Album Leaves, Op. 28 Grieg: 45 Selected Compositions, Bk. II
	Anitra's Dance, Op. 46, No. 3	GS P	Peer Gynt Suite I, Op. 46
	Ase's Death, Op. 46, No. 2		
	At Thy Feet, Op. 68, No. 3	GS P GS	Lyrical Pieces, Op. 68 Grieg: 45 Selected Compositions, Bk. I
	Bell Ringing, Op. 54, No. 6	GS P GS GS	Lyrical Pieces, Op. 54 Grieg: 45 Selected Compositions, Bk. I Published Separately
	Berceuse, Op. 38, No. 1	GS P K GS GS	Lyrical Pieces, Op. 38 Grieg; 45 Selected Compositions, Bk. I Selected Piano Solos by Romantic Composers, Vol. II
	Canon, Op. 38, No. 8	GS P K GS	Lyrical Pieces, Op. 38 Grieg: 45 Selected Compositions, Bk. II
	Dance Caprice, Op. 28, No. 3	GS P GS GS	Lyrical Pieces, Op. 28 Grieg: 45 Selected Compositions, Bk. I Published Separately
	Elegie, Op. 38, No. 6	GS P K GS	Lyrical Pieces, Op. 38 Grieg: 45 Selected Compositions, Bk. I
	Elegie, Op. 47, No. 7	GS P GS	Lyrical Pieces, Op. 47 Grieg: 45 Selected Compositions, Bk. II
	Elfin Dance, Op. 12, No. 4	GS P	Lyrical Pieces, Op. 12

Composer	Title	Publisher	Volume or Collection
GRIEG, E. (cont.)		K	
		GS	Grieg: 45 Selected Compositions, Bk. I
		GS	Master Series for the Young
		CF	Road to Piano Artistry, Vol. III (Scionti)
		GS	Published Separately
		Su	Piano Literature of the 17th, 18th and 19th Centuries, Bk. 4b (Clark)
	Erotik, Op. 43, No. 5	GS	Lyrical Pieces, Op. 43
		P	
		K	
		GS	Published Separately
	Folk-Song, Op. 12, No. 5	GS	Lyrical Pieces, Op. 12
		P	
		K	
		GS	Grieg: 45 Selected Compositions, Bk. I
		GS	Master Series for the Young
		He	A Treasury of Easy Classics (Abrams)
	Folk-Song, Op. 38, No. 2	GS	Lyrical Pieces, Op. 38
		P	
		K	
		GS	Grieg: 45 Selected Compositions, Bk. I
		GS	Master Series for the Young
	In My Native Country, Op. 43, No. 3	GS	Lyrical Pieces, Op. 43
		P	
		K	
		GS	Grieg: 45 Selected Compositions, Bk. I
	In the Hall of the Mountain King, Op. 46, No. 4	GS	Peer Gynt Suite I, Op. 46
		P	
		GS	Published Separately
	Little Bird, Op. 43, No. 4	GS	Lyrical Pieces, Op. 43
		P	
		K	
		CF	Road to Piano Artistry, Vol. IV (Scionti)
		GS	Published Separately
	Melody, Op. 38, No. 3	GS	Lyrical Pieces, Op. 38
		P	
		K	
		GS	Grieg: 45 Selected Compositions, Bk. II
	Melody, Op. 47, No. 3	GS	Lyrical Pieces, Op. 47
		P	
	Morning Mood, Op. 46, No. 1	GS	Peer Gynt Suite I, Op. 46
		P	
		GS	Published Separately
	Norwegian Bridal Pro- cession, Op. 19, No. 2	GS	Sketches of Norwegian Life, Op. 19
		P	
		GS	Grieg: 45 Selected Compositions, Bk. II
	Norwegian Dance, Op. 38, No. 4	GS	Lyrical Pieces, Op. 38
		P	
		K	

Composer	Title	Publisher	Volume or Collection
GRIEG, E. (cont.)	Norwegian Dance, Op. 47, No. 4	GS P	Lyrical Pieces, Op. 47
	Norwegian Melody, Op. 12, No. 6	GS P K GS GS	Lyrical Pieces, Op. 12 Grieg: 45 Selected Compositions, Bk. I Master Series for the Young
	Notturno, Op. 54, No. 4	GS P K GS GS	Lyrical Pieces, Op. 54 Grieg: 45 Selected Compositions, Bk. II Published Separately
	Papillons (Butterfly), Op. 43, No. 1	GS P K GS GS	Lyrical Pieces, Op. 43 Grieg: 45 Selected Compositions, Bk. I Published Separately
	Sailor's Song, Op. 68, No. 1	GS P GS GS	Lyrical Pieces, Op. 68 Master Series for the Young Published Separately
	Skip Dance, Op. 38, No. 5	GS P K GS	Lyrical Pieces, Op. 68 Master Series for the Young
	Solitary Traveller (Solitary Wanderer), Op. 43, No. 2	GS P K GS CF GS	Lyrical Pieces, Op. 43 Grieg: 45 Selected Compositions, Bk. I Road to Piano Artistry, Vol. VI (Scionti) Published Separately
	Solvejg's Songs, Op. 55, No. 4	GS P GS	Peer Gynt Suite II, Op. 55 Master Series for the Young
	Waltz, Op. 38, No. 7	GS P K GS GS	Lyrical Pieces, Op. 38 Grieg: 45 Selected Compositions, Bk. I Selected Piano Solos by Romantic Composers, Bk. III
GURLITT, C. (1820-1901)	Barcarolle, Op. 131, No. 22	GS	Twenty-four Melodious Studies, Op. 131
	Evening Piece, Op. 131, No. 20		
HELLER, S. (1813-1888)	At Evening, Op. 138	WR	Rediscovered Classics, Bk. 2 (Henderson)
	From "Fifty Selected Studies"	GS	Fifty Selected Studies, From Op. 45, 46, 47

Composer	Title	Publisher	Volume or Collection
HELLER, S. (cont.)	11. Interlude, Op. 47, No. 20		
	14. Tally-Ho, Op. 47, No. 18		
	17. Joyous Song, Op. 45, No. 4		
	19. Village Dance, Op. 45, No. 20		
	24. The Warrior's Song, Op. 45, No. 15		
	27. Spinning Song, Op. 45, No. 19		
	28. Sailing Along, Op. 45, No. 23		
	29. Wind in the Wheat- field, Op. 45, No. 24		
	30. Epilogue, Op. 45, No. 25		
	31. Without A Care, Op. 46, No. 1		
	33. The Bees, Op. 46, No. 5		
	36. Song Without Words, Op. 46, No. 8		
	37. The Spinning Top, Op. 46, No. 10		
	39. The Mountain Cas- cade, Op. 46, No. 12		
	40. Punchinello, Op. 46, No. 16		
	41. On the Riviera, Op. 46, No. 17		
	42. The Blacksmith, Op. 46, No. 18		
	43. In A Swing, Op. 46, No. 19		
	44. The New Bicycle, Op. 46, No. 21		
	45. Drummer Boy, Op. 46, No. 23		
	46. With Cap and Bells, Op. 46, No. 24		
	47. Boat Song, Op. 46, No. 25		
	48. Storm at Sea, Op. 46, No. 26		
	49. The Town Crier, Op. 46, No. 27		
	From "Thirty Progressive Studies," Op. 46	GS	Thirty Progressive Studies, Op. 46
	1. Without A Care	R	
	4. Shooting the Rapids	K	
	5. The Bees	P	
	8. Song Without Words		

Composer	Title	Publisher	Volume or Collection
HELLER, S. (cont.)	9. Playing Tag		
	10. The Spinning Top		
	12. The Mountain Cascade		
	14. Gaiety		
	15. Idilio		
	16. Punchinello		
	17. On the Riviera		
	18. The Blacksmith		
	19. In A Swing		
	20. Dwarf's March		
	21. The New Bicycle		
	23. Drummer Boy		
	24. With Cap and Bells		
	25. Boat Song		
	26. Storm at Sea		
	27. The Town Crier		
	28. Smoothly Sailing		
	29. Anticipation		
	From "Twenty Five Melodious Studies," Op. 45	GS R K P	Twenty Five Melodious Studies, Op. 45
	3. Up and Down the Steps		
	4. Joyous Song		
	6. Shadow Waltz		
	11. Caprice		
	12. Sternness		
	13. Waltz		
	15. The Warrior's Song		
	17. Novelette		
	19. Spinning Song		
	20. Village Dance		
	21. Gnomes		
	22. The Harp		
	23. Sailing Along		
	24. Wind in the Wheatfield		
	25. Epilogue		
	From "Twenty Five Studies," Op. 47	GS R K P	Twenty Five Studies, Op. 47
	8. Spinning Wheel		
	18. Tally-Ho		
	20. Interlude		
	2 . Express Train		
	24. Serenity		
	25. Country Festival		
	Preludes, Op. 81 (Complete)	GS P	Twenty-four Preludes, Op. 81
	Prelude in C-sharp Minor, Op. 81, No. 10	WR	Rediscovered Classics, Bk. 4 (Henderson)
	Prelude in D Minor (Sailing Along), Op. 45, No. 23	CF GS	Road to Piano Artistry, Vol. VII (Scionti) Twenty Five Melodious Studies, Op. 45

Composer	Title	Publisher	Volume or Collection
HELLER, S. (cont.)		P R K GS	Fifty Selected Studies from Op. 45, 46, 47 (No. 28)
	Remembrance, Op. 82, No. 3	WR	Rediscovered Classics, Bk. 2 (Henderson)
	Study in A (Spinning Wheel) Op. 47, No. 8	GS R GS K P	Selected Piano Solos by Romantic Composers, Bk. I Twenty Five Studies, Op. 47
	Warrior's Song, Op. 45 No. 15	GS GS R P K GS	Selected Piano Solos by Romantic Composers, Bk. III Twenty Five Studies, Op. 47 Fifty Selected Studies from Op. 45, 46, 47 (No. 24)
HUMMEL, J. N. (1778-1837)	Rondo in C	P	Sonatinen Album, Vol. II
JENSEN, A. (1837-1879)	Dedication, Op. 33	H	Contemporaries of Schumann
	Hungarian Melody, Op. 33, No. 13	WR	Rediscovered Classics, Bk. 4 (Henderson)
	Lied, Op. 33, No. 10	H B	Contemporaries of Schumann Hours with the Masters, Bk. IV
	Longing, Op. 8, No. 5	B	Hours with the Masters, Bk. IV
	Peaceful Afternoon, Op. 17, No. 7	CF	Road to Piano Artistry, Vol. V
KUHLAU, F. (1786-1832)	Rondo in A, Op. 40, No. 2	GS	Thirty Two Sonatinas and Rondos
	Sonatina in A Minor, Op. 88, No. 3 Allegro con affetto Andantino Allegro burlesco	GS GS	Kuhlau Sonatinas, Bk. II Thirty Two Sonatinas and Rondos
	Sonatina in C, Op. 20, No. 1 Allegro Andante Rondo	GS GS GS P	Kuhlau Sonatinas, Bk. I Album of Sonatinas Thirty Two Sonatinas and Rondos Sonatinen Album, Vol. I
	Sonatina in C, Op. 55, No. 3 Allegro con spirito Allegretto grazioso	GS GS GS P	Kuhlau Sonatinas, Bk. I Album of Sonatinas Thirty Two Sonatinas and Rondos Sonatinen Album, Vol. I

Composer	Title	Publisher	Volume or Collection
KUHLAU, F. (cont.)	Sonatina in C, Op. 55 No. 6 Allegro maestoso Menuet	GS P	Kuhlau Sonatinas, Bk. I Sonatinen Album, Vol. II
	Sonatina in C, Op. 88, No. 1 Allegro Andantino Rondo	GS GS P P	Kuhlau Sonatinas, Bk. II Selected Sonatinas, Bk. I Sonatinen Album, Vol. II Sonatinen Vorstüfe, Vol. II
	Sonatina in D, Op. 55, No. 5 Tempo di Marcia Vivace assai	GS GS P	Kuhlau Sonatinas, Bk. I Thirty Two Sonatinas and Rondos Sonatinen Album, Vol. II
	Sonatina in F, Op. 20, No. 3 Allegro quasi presto Rondo	GS GS GS P	Kuhlau Sonatinas, Bk. I Selected Sonatinas, Bk. II Album of Sonatinas Sonatinen Album, Vol. I
	Sonatina in F, Op. 55, No. 4 Allegro ma non tanto Andante con espressione Alla Polacca	GS GS P	Kuhlau Sonatinas, Bk. I Thirty Two Sonatinas and Rondos Sonatinen Album, Vol. II
	Sonatina in F, Op. 88, No. 4 Allegro molto Andante con moto Alla Polacca	GS	Kuhlau Sonatinas, Bk. II
	Sonatina in G, Op. 20, No. 2 Allegro Adagio e sostenuto Allegro scherzando	GS GS GS P	Kuhlau Sonatinas, Bk. I Album of Sonatinas Selected Sonatinas, Bk. II Sonatinen Album, Vol. I
	Sonatina in G, Op. 88, No. 2 Allegro assai Andante cantabile Rondo	GS GS P	Kuhlau Sonatinas, Bk. II Thirty Two Sonatinas and Rondos Sonatinen Album, Vol. II
LISZT, F. (1811-1886)	Consolation in E, No. 1	GS GS He PP	Liszt: Consolations; Liebesträume Selected Piano Solos by Romantic Composers, Bk. III A Little Treasury of Classics, Bk. IV (Lambert) Hundred Best Short Classics, Bk. III
MACDOWELL, E. (1861-1908)	Alla Tarantella, Op. 39, No. 2	BMC Su	Twelve Etudes, Op. 39 Published Separately
	Hunting Song, Op. 39, No. 1	BMC	Twelve Etudes, Op. 39
	From "New England Idylls," Op. 62	GS K	New England Idylls, Op. 62

Composer	Title	Publisher	Volume or Collection
MACDOWELL, E. (cont.)	2. Midsummer		
	3. Midwinter		
	4. With Sweet Lavender		
	5. In Deep Woods		
	6. Indian Idyll		
	7. To an Old White Pine		
	8. From Puritan Days		
	9. From A Log Cabin		
	From "Woodland Sketches," Op. 51	AMP GS K	Woodland Sketches, Op. 51
	3. At An Old Trysting Place	M	
	5. From An Indian Lodge	Su	Piano Literature of the 17th, 18th and 19th Centuries, Bk. 5b (Clark)
	6. To A Water-Lily		
	7. From Uncle Remus		
	8. A Deserted Farm		
	10. Told At Sunset		
	Romance, Op. 39, No. 3	BMC	Twelve Etudes, Op. 39
	Scotch Poem (Gedichte nach Heinrich Heine, Op. 31, No. 2)	GS	Published Separately
	Sea Pieces, Op. 55	Su GS	Sea Pieces, Op. 55
	1. To The Sea		
	2. From A Wandering Iceberg		
	3. A.D. 1620		
	4. Starlight		
	6. From the Depths		
	7. Nautilus		
	8. In Midocean		
MENDELSSOHN, F. (1809-1847)	Allegro in G, Op. 72, No. 1	P GS	Six Pieces for Children, Op. 72
		GS	Master Series for the Young
		He	A Treasury of Easy Classics (Abrams)
		A	Beringer's School of Easy Classics: Mendelssohn
		PP	Hundred Best Short Classics, Bk. III
	Allegretto in G, Op. 72, No. 3	P GS	Six Pieces for Children, Op. 72
		GS	Master Series for the Young
		A	Beringer's School of Easy Classics: Mendelssohn
		PP	Hundred Best Short Classics, Bk. II
	Andante con moto in D, Op. 72, No. 4	P GS	Six Pieces for Children, Op. 72
		GS	Master Series for the Young
		A	Beringer's School of Easy Classics: Mendelssohn

Composer	Title	Publisher	Volume or Collection
MENDELSSOHN, F. (cont.)	Andante sostenuto in E-flat, Op. 72, No. 2	P GS	Six Pieces for Children, Op. 72
		GS	Master Series for the Young
		A	Beringer's School of Easy Classics: Mendelssohn
		PP	Hundred Best Short Classics, Bk. II
		CF	Road to Piano Artistry, Vol. IV (Scionti)
	Boat Song, Op. 102, No. 7	GS P Wo	Songs Without Words
		GS	Master Series for the Young
	Confidence, Op. 19, No. 4	GS P Wo	Songs Without Words
		GS	Master Series for the Young
		A	Beringer's School of Easy Classics: Mendelssohn
		GS	Selected Piano Solos by Romantic Composers, Bk. II
	Consolation, Op. 30, No. 3	GS Wo P	Songs Without Words
		PP	Hundred Best Short Classics, Bk. II
		GS	Master Series for the Young
		A	Beringer's School of Easy Classics: Mendelssohn
	Faith, Op. 102, No. 6	GS P Wo	Songs Without Words
		GS	Master Series for the Young
	Hope, Op. 38, No. 4	GS P Wo	Songs Without Words
		GS	Master Series for the Young
		GS	Selected Piano Solos by Romantic Composers, Bk. II
	Morning Song, Op. 62, No. 4	GS P Wo	Songs Without Words
		GS	Selected Piano Solos by Romantic Composers, Bk. II
	Regrets, Op. 19, No. 2	GS P Wo	Songs Without Words
		GS	Selected Piano Solos by Romantic Composers, Bk. II
		B	Hours with the Masters, Bk. IV
		GS	Master Series for the Young
	Sadness of Soul, Op. 53, No. 4	GS P Wo	Songs Without Words

Composer	Title	Publisher	Volume or Collection
MENDELSSOHN. F. (cont.)	Shepherd's Complaint, Op. 67, No. 5	GS P Wo	Songs Without Words
	Spring Song, Op. 62, No. 6	GS P Wo GS GS	Songs Without Words Master Series for the Young Introduction to Piano Classics, Vol. III (Mirovitch)
	Tarantella, Op. 102, No. 3	GS P Wo GS	Songs Without Words Introduction to Piano Classics, Vol. III (Mirovitch)
	Venetian Boat Song I, Op. 19, No. 6	GS P Wo GS GS A	Songs Without Words Master Series for the Young Introduction to Piano Classics, Vol. III (Mirovitch) Beringer's School of Easy Classics: Mendelssohn
	Venetian Boat Song, II, Op. 30, No. 6	GS P Wo	Songs Without Words
SCHUBERT. F. (1797-1828)	Allegretto (No. 2)	M	Six Rare Piano Pieces (Mirovitch)
	Andante (No. 1)		
	Deutsch Tänze, Op. 33 (Complete)	P GS	Schubert Dances
	1. A Major	H	Easiest Original Pieces
	2. D Major	H	Easiest Original Pieces
	3. B-flat	H	Easiest Original Pieces
	5. D Major	H He	Easiest Original Pieces A Treasury of Easy Classics (Abrams)
	7. B-flat	H Su	Easiest Original Pieces Piano Literature of the 17th, 18th and 19th Centuries, Bk. 4b (Clark)
	9. C Major	Su	Piano Literature of the 17th, 18th and 19th Centuries, Bk. 4b (Clark)
	15. A-Flat		
	Ecossaises, Op. 18a (Complete)	P GS GS	Schubert Dances Introduction to Piano Classics, Vol. II (Mirovitch)
	1. A-flat Major	Su	Piano Literature of the 17th, 18th and 19th Centuries, Bk. 5b (Clark)
	2. D Major	He	A Treasury of Easy Classics (Abrams)
	3. G Major	GS	Master Series for the Young
	Ländler, Op. 171	P GS	Schubert Dances

Composer	Title	Publisher	Volume or Collection
SCHUBERT. F. (cont.)	Ländler, Op. posth.	P GS	Schubert Dances
	Ländler in A Minor (From Op. posth.)	He	A Little Treasury of Classics, Bk. II (Lambert)
	Ländler in B-flat		
	Ländler, Op. 67 (Hommage aux Belles Viennoises)	P GS	Schubert Dances
	Menuette, Op. posth. (Eight Minuets) (Complete)	P GS	Schubert Dances
	1. F Major	H	Easiest Original Pieces
	2. C Major	GS	Introduction to Piano Classics, Vol. II (Mirovitch)
	4. F Major	GS	Introduction to Piano Classics, Vol. II (Mirovitch)
	Scherzo in B-flat	P	Sonatinen Album, Vol. I
	Two Country Dances (From Op. 171)	H	Easiest Original Pieces
	Waltzes, Op. 9a (18 Waltzes) (Complete)	P GS	Schubert Dances
	1. A-flat	H GS CF Su	Easiest Original Pieces Master Series for the Young Road to Piano Artistry, Vol. III Piano Literature of the 17th, 18th and 19th Centuries, Bk. 5b (Clark)
	2. A-flat	H GS CF Su WR	Easiest Original Pieces Master Series for the Young Road to Piano Artistry, Vol. III (Scionti) Piano Literature of the 17th, 18th and 19th Centuries, Bk. 5b (Clark) Rediscovered Classics, Bk. 3 (Henderson)
	(In key of G)	BH	From Ancient to Modern (Rowley)
	3. A-flat	GS CF	Master Series for the Young Road to Piano Artistry, Vol. III (Scionti)
	6. A-flat	Su	Piano Literature of the 17th, 18th and 19th Centuries, Bk. 5b (Clark)
	11. A-flat	Co	The Solo Book, Vol. III (Zeetlin and Goldberger)
	Waltzes, Op. 9b (18 Waltzes Complete)	P GS	Schubert Dances
	1. G Major	Su	Piano Literature of the 17th, 18th and 19th Centuries, Bk. 3 (Clark)
	3. G Major	Su	Piano Literature of the 17th, 18th and 19th Centuries, Bk. 3 (Clark)
	Waltz in B, Op. 18a, No. 10	P GS	Schubert Dances
	Waltz in B Minor, Op. 18a, No. 9		
	Waltz in D, Op. 18a, No. 5	P GS	Schubert Dances

Composer	Title	Publisher	Volume or Collection
SCHUBERT, F. (cont.)		GS	Introduction to Piano Classics, Vol. III (Mirovitch)
		Su	Piano Literature of the 17th, 18th and 19th Centuries, Bk. 4b (Clark)
	Waltz in E-flat, Op. 18a, No. 6	P GS	Schubert Dances
	Waltz in G, Op. 18a, No. 4	P GS	Schubert Dances
		GS	Introduction to Piano Classics, Vol. III (Mirovitch)
	Waltz in G-flat, Op. 18a, No. 7	P GS	Schubert Dances
	Waltzes, Op. 50 (12 Valses sentimentales)	P	Schubert Dances
	4. D Major	He	A Treasury of Easy Classics (Abrams)
	5. D Major	He	A Treasury of Easy Classics (Abrams)
		GS	Master Series for the Young
	12. A-flat	A	Beringer's School of Easy Classics: Schubert
	Waltzes, Op. 91a (12 Grätzer Walzer)	P GS	Schubert Dances
	Waltzes (Selected) Sets I, II and IV	JF	Schubert Dances (Maier)
SCHUMANN, R. (1810-1856)	Andante con espressione, Op. 68, No. 26	GS P Co	Album for the Young, Op. 68
		GS	Master Series for the Young
	Cradle Song, Op. 124, No. 6	GS P	Album Leaves, Op. 124
		K	Complete Works, Vol. VI
		GS	Master Series for the Young
		H	Easiest Original Pieces
		P	Sonatinen Album, Vol. II
	Curious Story, Op. 15, No. 2	AMP GS P	Scenes from Childhood, Op. 15
		K	Complete Works, Vol. III
		GS	Master Series for the Young
	Echoes from the Theater, Op. 68, No. 25	GS P K Co	Album for the Young, Op. 68
	From Foreign Lands and Peoples, Op. 15, No. 1	GS AMP P	Scenes from Childhood, Op. 15
		K	Complete Works, Vol. III
		GS	Master Series for the Young
		PP	Hundred Best Short Classics, Bk. IV

Composer	Title	Publisher	Volume or Collection
SCHUMANN, R. (cont.)	Important Event, Op. 15, No. 6	P GS AMP	Scenes from Childhood, Op. 15
		K	Complete Works, Vol. III
	In Memoriam, Op. 68, No. 28	GS P K Co	Album for the Young, Op. 68
		GS	Master Series for the Young
	Italian Sailor's Song, Op. 68, No. 36	GS P K Co	Album for the Young, Op. 68
		GS	Master Series for the Young
		GS	Selected Piano Solos by Romantic Composers, Bk. II
	Lento assai, Op. 68, No. 30	GS P K Co	Album for the Young, Op. 68
	Lento espressivo, Op. 68, No. 21		
	May Charming May, Op. 68, No. 13	GS P K Co	Album for the Young, Op. 68
		A	Beringer's School of Easy Classics: Schumann
		B	Hours with the Masters, Bk. V
		PP	Hundred Best Short Classics, Bk. IV
	Mignon, Op. 68, No. 35	GS P K Co	Album for the Young, Op. 68
	New Year's Eve, Op. 68, No. 43	GS	Published Separately
	Norse Song, Op. 68, No. 4	GS P K Co	Album for the Young, Op. 68
		GS	Introduction to Piano Classics, Vol. II (Mirovitch)
		GS	Selected Piano Solos by Romantic Composers, Bk. II
		Su	Piano Literature of the 17th, 18th and 19th Centuries, Bk. 5b (Clark)
		GS	Published Separately
	Roaming in the Morning, Op. 68, No. 17	GS P K	Album for the Young, Op. 68

Composer	Title	Publisher	Volume or Collection
SCHUMANN, R. (cont.)		Co	
		GS	Master Series for the Young
	Roundelay, Op. 68, No. 22	GS	Album for the Young, Op. 68
		P	
		K	
		Co	
	Sailor's Song, Op. 68, No. 37		
	Scheherazade, Op. 68, No. 32		
	Solitary Flowers, Op. 82, No. 2	GS	Forest Scenes, Op. 82
		AMP	
		P	
		K	Complete Works, Vol. V
		H	Easiest Original Pieces
	Sonata for the Young, Op. 118, No. 1	GS	Three Sonatas for the Young People, Op. 118
		K	Complete Works, Vol. VI
		P	Complete Works, Vol. IV
	Allegro Theme and Variations Doll's Cradle Song Rondoletto		
	Song in Canon Form, Op. 68, No. 27	GS	Album for the Young, Op. 68
		P	
		K	
		Co	
	Spring Song, Op. 68, No. 15		
	Strange Man, Op. 68, No. 29	GS	Album for the Young, Op. 68
		P	
		K	
		Co	
		GS	Selected Piano Solos by Romantic Composers, Bk. II
	Vintage Time, Op. 68, No. 33	GS	Album for the Young, Op. 68
		P	
		K	
		Co	
	Waltz, Op. 124, No. 4	GS	Album Leaves, Op. 124
		P	
		K	Complete Works, Vol. VI
		H	Easiest Original Pieces
		A	Beringer's School of Easy Classics: Schumann
		PP	Hundred Best Short Classics, Bk. II
		B	Hours with the Masters, Bk. III
		Su	Piano Literature of the 17th, 18th and 19th Centuries, Bk. 5b (Clark)

Composer	Title	Publisher	Volume or Collection
SCHUMANN, R. (cont.)	Winter-Time I, Op. 68, No. 38	GS P Co K	Album for the Young, Op. 68
	Winter-Time II, Op. 68, No. 39		
TSCHAIKOWSKY, P. (1840-1893)	A Song of Sadness, Op. 40, No. 2	GS	Master Series for the Young
	April-Snowdrop, Op. 37a, No. 4	GS PP GS P	The Seasons, Op. 37a Hundred Best Short Classics, Bk. III Introduction to Piano Classics, Vol. II The Seasons, Op. 37a
	Chanson Triste	PP	Hundred Best Short Classics, Bk. V
	German Song, Op. 39, No. 17	GS P GS Su	Album for the Young, Op. 39 Master Series for the Young Piano Literature of the 17th, 18th and 19th Centuries, Bk. 4b (Clark)
	January--By the Hearth, Op. 37a, No. 1	GS P	The Seasons, Op. 37a
	May--Starlit Night, Op. 37a, No. 5		
	October--Autumn Song, Op. 37a, No. 10		
	Polka, Op. 39, No. 10	GS P GS	Album for the Young, Op. 39 Master Series for the Young
	Russian Dance, Op. 39, No. 13	GS P GS	Album for the Young, Op. 39 Master Series for the Young
	Song Without Words, Op. 40, No. 6	GS	Master Series for the Young
	The Hobby Horse, Op. 39, No. 3	GS P	Album for the Young, Op. 39
	The Nurse's Tale, Op. 39, No. 19		
	The Witch, Op. 39, No. 20	GS P He Su	Album for the Young, Op. 39 A Treasury of Easy Classics (Abrams) Piano Literature of the 17th, 18th and 19th Centuries, Bk. 5b (Clark)
	Waltz, Op. 39, No. 8	GS P GS He	Album for the Young, Op. 39 Master Series for the Young A Treasury of Easy Classics (Abrams)

Composer	Title	Publisher	Volume or Collection
TSCHAIKOWSKY, P. (cont.)	Winter Morning, Op. 39, No. 2	GS P	Album for the Young, Op. 39
		GS	Master Series for the Young
WEBER, C. (1786-1826)	Andante with Variations, Op. 3, No. 4	GS	Master Series for the Young
	Andantino, Op. 10, No. 2	GS	Master Series for the Young
	Minuet, Op. 3, No. 3	GS	Master Series for the Young
	Moderato (From Sonatina, Op. 3, No. 1)	He GS	Little Treasury of Sonatinas, Bk. II Master Series for the Young
	Theme (From Invitation to the Dance, Op. 65)	GS	Master Series for the Young
	Waltz in A	GS	Master Series for the Young
	Waltz in C		

Composer	Title	Publisher	Volume or Collection
BARTÓK, BÉLA (1881-1945)	Bagatelles Nos. 1, 3, 4, 6	BH	Fourteen Bagatelles, Op. 6
	Bear Dance	K	Ten Easy Pieces for Piano
	Dirge, Op. 8b, No. 1	BH	Four Dirges, Op. 8b
	From "Mikrokosmos"	BH	Mikrokosmos
	Vol. IV Variations on a Folk-tune Melody		
	Vol. V Boating Peasant Dance A Village Joke Merry Andrew		
	Rumanian Folk Dances Nos. 1, 2, 3, 4	BH	Rumanian Folk Dances
BARVINSKY (1888-)	A Light Ram	L	Children's Piano Pieces by Soviet Composers
BLOCH, ERNEST (1880-1959)	Chanty (From "Poems of the Sea")	GS	51 Piano Pieces from the Modern Repertoire
BRIDGE, FRANK (1844-1924)	From "Miniature Pastorals" 4. Allegro giusto 5. Andante con moto 6. Allegro ma non troppo	BH	Miniature Pastorals for Piano: 2nd Set
CARVAJAL, ARMANDO (?)	March	MMC	Meet Modern Music, Pt. II
CASELLA, ALFREDO (1883-1947)	Children's Pieces 1. Preludio 2. Canon 3. Valse Diatonique 4. Bolero 5. In Honor of Clementi 6. Siciliano 7. Giga 8. Minuetto 9. Carillon 10. Berceuse 11. Galop Final	AMP	Eleven Children's Pieces

Composer	Title	Publisher	Volume or Collection
CASTRO, JOSÈ MARIA (1909-)	Pequeña Marcha	EAM	Published Separately
CATURLA. ALEJANDRO (1906-1940)	Piece in Cuban Style, in F Minor	CF	Published Separately
CHAVEZ, CARLOS (1899-)	From "Ten Preludes" 1. Andantino espressivo 2. Vivace 3. Poco mosso 5. Cantabile 6. Calmo 9. Moderato. molto cantabile	GS	Ten Preludes
COPLAND. AARON (1900-)	The Young Pioneers	CF CF	Masters of Our Day; 18 Solos in the Contemporary Idiom Published Separately
COWELL. HENRY (1897-)	The Harper-Minstrel Sings	CF CF	Masters of Our Day; 18 Solos in the Contemporary Idiom Published Separately
FICHER. JACABO (1896-)	Cancion Triste	So	Published Separately
FREED, ISADORE (1900-1960)	A Lake Song	CF	Published Separately
FULEIHAN, ANIS (1900-)	Short Pieces 1. Casual Walk 2. Showing Off	So	Five Very Short Pieces for Talented Young Bipeds
	The Bailiff's Daughter	CF	Published Separately
GIANNEO, LUIS (1897-)	From "Petites Pièces" 2. Chanson A Bercer 3. Marche Des Petits Soldats 4. Valse Sentimentale	E	Cinq Petites Pièces
	From "Music for Children" 1. Prelude and Fugue 3. Zapateado 4. Argentinian Air 7. The Little Dark-haired Girl 8. Folk Song 9. Indian Lullaby 10. Little Dance Song	EAM	Musica Para Ninos

Composer	Title	Publisher	Volume or Collection
GINASTERA, ALBERTO (1916-)	From "12 American Preludes," Vol. I 2. Sadness 4. Vidala 5. In The First Pentatonic Mode 6. Tribute to Roberto Garcia	CF	12 American Preludes, Vol. I
	From "12 American Preludes," Vol. II 8. Tribute to Juan José Castro	CF	12 American Preludes, Vol. II
GLIÉRE, REINHOLD (1875-1926)	In the Fields, Op. 34, No. 7 (From "Characteristic Pieces for Young People")	W	Modern Russian Piano Music
	Mazurka	SG	Russian Piano Classics (Tapper)
	Melodie in A-flat	WR	Rediscovered Classics, Bk. 4 (Henderson)
	Serenade, Op. 34, No. 19	W	Modern Russian Piano Music
GOEDICKE, ALEXANDER (1877-)	Petrushka	SG	Russian Piano Classics (Tapper)
GOOSSENS, EUGENE (1893-1962)	"Kaleidoscope," Op. 18 3. Hurdy Gurdy Man 8. The Old Music Box 9. The Clock Work Dancer 10. Lament for Departed Doll 11. A Merry Party	C M M	Kaleidoscope, Op. 18 Published Separately Published Separately
GOULD, MORTON (1913-)	Corn-Cob (From "Americano")	CF	Published Separately
GRANADOS, ENRIQUE (1867-1916)	The Last Pavane Theme and Two Variations	MMC	Meet Modern Music, Pt. II
GREEN, RAY (1909-)	Rhapsodic Interlude	AME	Published Separately
GRETCHANINOFF, ALEXANDER (1864-1956)	Largo	Sch	The New Piano Book, Vol. II
GROVLEZ, GABRIEL (1879-1944)	From "A Child's Garden" 4. Chanson D'Ancêtre 5. Chanson Pour Faire Danser En Ronds Les Petits Enfants	C	A Child's Garden

Composer	Title	Publisher	Volume or Collection

HARRIS, ROY
(1898-   )
	Little Suite
	  1. Bells
	  2. Sad News
	  3. Children At Play
	  4. Slumber
		GS
		GS
			Little Suite
			51 Piano Pieces from the Modern Repertoire

HERRATE, MANUEL (1924-)	Andante	EV	6 Modern Guatemalan Composers
IBERT, JACQUES (1890-1962)	La Meneuse de tortues d'or, No. 1 Le palais abandonné, No. 6 Le vieux mendiant, No. 3	Le	Histoires

KABALEVSKY,
DMITRI
(1904-   )
	Variations, Op. 40, No. 1
	  in D
	
	Variations, Op. 40, No. 2,
	  in A Minor
		L	Variations, Op. 40

KHACHATURIAN,
ARAM
(1903-   )
	From "Adventures of Ivan"
	  4. Ivan Goes to A Party
	  5. Ivan Is Very Busy
	  6. Ivan and Natasha
	  7. Ivan's Hobby Horse
	  8. A Tale of Strange
	     Lands
		L	Adventures of Ivan

MENOTTI,
GIAN-CARLO
(1911-   )
	From "Poemetti"
	  6. The Brook
	  7. The Shepherd
	  8. Nocturne
	  9. The Stranger's Dance
	 10. Winter Wind
		R	Poemetti

MIASKOWSKY, NIKOLAI (1881-1951)	Elegiac Mood The Hunter's Call In Ancient Style, Op. 43, No. 4	L W	Children's Piano Pieces by Soviet Composers Modern Russian Piano Music

MILHAUD, DARIUS
(1892-   )
	Suite of 15 Pieces
	
	Two Pieces from "The
	  Child Loves"
	  4. Mother
	  5. Life
	
	Une Journée (One Day)
	  1. Dawn
	  2. Morning
	  3. Noon
	  4. Afternoon
	  5. Twilight
		EV
		
		MMC
			The Household Muse
			
			Une Journée

Composer	Title	Publisher	Volume or Collection

MOORE, DOUGLAS
(1893-   )
	From "Suite for Piano"
	  1. Air
	  3. Barn Dance
		CF	Published Separately

PALMGREN, SELIM (1878-1951)	Roundelay, Op. 79, No. 4	CF	Published Separately
	White Lilies	SG	Published Separately
PAZ, JUAN C. (1897-)	At the Coast of Parana	CF	Published Separately

PINTO, OCTAVIO
(1890-1950)
	From "Memories of Child-
	    hood"
	  3. March Little Soldier
	  4. Sleeping Time
		GS	Memories of Childhood

PISK, PAUL A. (1893-)	From the Ozarks	CF	Masters of Our Day
POULENC, FRANCIS (1889-1963)	Valse, in C	AMP	Published Separately
RAKOFF, NICOLAS (1908-)	Novelette	W	Modern Russian Piano Music
REBIKOV, VLADIMIR (1866-1920)	The Fairy The Mother By the Cradle	GS	Silhouettes, Op. 31
	Witches Dance	Sch	Piano Album No. II

REGER, MAX
(1873-1916)
	From "Jugend--Album II"
	  1. Bange Frage
	  2. Fast zu keck
	  3. Erster Streit
	  4. Was die Grossmutter
	     erzählt
	  5. A la Gigue
	  6. Nordischer Tänz
	  7. Versöhnung
		Sch	Jugend--Album II

RHENE-BATON
(1879-1940)
	From "Album Rose"
	  1. Petite Mélodie
	  2. Bluette
	  3. Intermezzo
	  4. Petit Choral
	  5. Vieille Romance
	  6. Musette
		E	Album Rose

ROLDÁN, AMADEO (1900-1939)	The "Diablito" Dances	CF	Published Separately
ROZSA, MIKLOS (1907-)	Berceuse from "Kaleido- scope", Op. 19	AMP	Published Separately

Composer	Title	Publisher	Volume or Collection
ROZSA, MIKLOS (cont.)	Chinese Carillon, from "Kaleidoscope", Op. 19	AMP	Published Separately
	March, from "Kaleidoscope", Op. 19	AMP	Published Separately
SAMINSKY, LAZARE (1882-)	Fooling with Scottie, Op. 45, No. 6	CF	Published Separately
	Mischief, Op. 45, No. 5	CF	Published Separately
SANJUAN, PEDRO (1886-)	Reflections of Susanne	CF	Published Separately
SATIE, ERIK (1866-1925)	Gymnopedie No. I	S	Published Separately
		M	Published Separately
		He	Published Separately
	Gymnopedie No. II	S	Published Separately
		M	Published Separately
		GS	51 Piano Pieces from the Modern Repertoire
	Gymnopedie No. III	S	Published Separately
		M	Published Separately
	Gnossienne No. 1	M	Published Separately
SCHMITT, FLORENT (1870-)	Rocking	CF	Published Separately
	Waltzing	CF	Published Separately
SCHUMAN, WILLIAM (1910-)	From 3 Piano Moods		
	Lyrical	TP	Published Separately
	Pensive	TP	Published Separately
SCOTT, CYRIL (1879-)	A Ballad Told At Candlelight	Sch	Miniatures
		Sch	The New Piano Book, Vol. II
	Dawn	Sch	Impressions from the Jungle Book
	Morning Song In The Jungle		
	The Jungle		
	To An Old Miniature	Sch	Miniatures
SESSIONS, ROGER (1896-)	March	CF	Masters of Our Day; 18 Solos in the Contemporary Idiom
		CF	Published Separately
	Scherzino	CF	Published Separately
SÉVÉRAC, D. de (1873-1921)	En Vacances—Series I Invocation to Schumann Grandma's Caresses The Little Girls from Next Door In Chapel	S	En Vacances—Series I

Composer	Title	Publisher	Volume or Collection
SÉVÉRAC, D. de (cont.)	In Powdered Wig and Hoop Skirt		
	Games in the Park		
SHEBALIN, V. (1902-)	Meditation, Op. 12, No. 3	W	Modern Russian Piano Music
SHEPHERD, ARTHUR (1880-1958)	The Gay Promenade	CF	Masters of Our Day
SIBELIUS, JAN (1865-1957)	Evening Calm, Op. 46, No. 2	BMC	From The Land of Thousand Lakes
	Olden Days, Op. 46, No. 4		
	Pastorale, Op. 46, No. 5		
	Solitude, Op. 50, No. 3		
SIEGMEISTER, ELIE (1909-)	From "The Children's Day" 3. Playing Clown 4. On A Golden Afternoon 5. Catching Butterflies 6. Bedtime Story	L	The Children's Day
SLAVENSKI, JOSIP (1865-1930)	Slawischer Tanz	Sch	The New Piano Book, Vol. III
STARER, ROBERT (1924-)	Seven Vignettes 1. Fanfare 2. Song Without Words 3. Jig-Saw 4. The Interrupted Waltz 5. Chorale 6. The Camel and the Moon 7. Toccata	L	Seven Vignettes
TANSMAN, ALEXANDRE (1897-)	From "Petite Suite" 2. Berceuse 4. Petite chanson polonaise 6. Caprice	AMP	Petite Suite
	Hide and Seek	E	Pour les Enfants, Set IV
	Marche Militaire		
	Music of Bali		
	Procession	L S	Piano Miniatures
	Toccata	AMP	Ten Diversions for the Young Pianist

Composer	Title	Publisher	Volume or Collection
TANSMAN, ALEXANDRE (cont.)	From "Recreations" Game In Modo Bachico	Su	Recreations
TAYLOR, DEEMS (1885-)	The Smugglers	CF	Masters of Our Day; 18 Solos in the Contemporary Idiom
		CF	Published Separately
TCHÉREPNINE, ALEXANDRE (1899-)	From "Pour petits et grands" Set I 2. Le Farceur 3. La Mélodieuse 4. Les Contrastes 6. La Babillarde Set II 1. L'Affligée 2. L'Ibérienne 4. La Dévouée	D	Pour petits et grands
	The Hour of Death	L	Expressions, Op. 81
	From "les Juenes au Piano," Vol. I 2. Les petits poussins 4. Le jolie papillon 6. Le petit chien et la vilaine mouche	E	Vol. I—Mirielle Et Les Animaux
	From "les Juenes au Piano," Vol. III 1. Notre-Dame 7. Pigalle 8. Rond-Point des Champs Elysées	E	Vol. III—L'Autobus Imaginaire
THOMSON, VIRGIL (1896-)	Piano Sonata, No. 4 Allegro Adagio Vivace	EV	Piano Sonata, No. 4
TOCH, ERNST (1887-)	From "Echos of a Small Town" 3. Oh, If I Only Had . . .! 4. On the Way to School 5. The Hand-Organ Man 7. Poor Child 9. Full of Fun 10. Lonesome 11. Following the Band 12. Downtown 14. Vacation	AMP	Echos of a Small Town

Composer	Title	Publisher	Volume or Collection
VILLA-LOBOS, HEITOR (1887-1960)	Five Pieces 1. The Child's Dream 2. The Hunchback 3. The Crab 4. The Little Dove 5. Let Us Go Over the Mountain, O Calunga	MP	Five Pieces on Popular Children's Folktunes of Brazil, Album VI
	Francette et Piá 6. Piá Went to War	E	Published Separately
	From "Guia prático," Album I 1. Dawn 2. Full Tide 3. The Rose-bush 4. Little Lame Girl 5. The Strings of a Violin	Co	Guia prático, Album I
	From "Guia prático," Album VIII 1. Oh, Lemon 2. Goodness 3. Poor Blind Woman 4. Father Francisco 5. Fly! Little Bird 6. Farmer's Daughters 7. Little White Dress	VL	Guia práctico--Album VIII
	Album IX 1. The Little Orange Tree 3. Circle Dance 5. Constant 6. The Castle	VL	Guia prático--Album IX
WAXMAN, FRANZ (1906-)	From "The Charm Bracelet" 3. The Little Soldier 4. The Golden Heart 5. The Pony	L	The Charm Bracelet

SECTION IV

LOWER ADVANCED

GRADES VII AND VIII

MUSIC OF THE SIXTEENTH, SEVENTEENTH
AND EIGHTEENTH CENTURIES

Composer	Title	Publisher	Volume or Collection
ARNE, T. A. (1710-1778)	Allegretto in D Minor	A	Beringer's School of Easy Classics: Old English and French Masters
	Allegro (From Sonata in A)	CF B	Classic Sonatas (Podolsky) Hours with the Masters, Bk. V
	Sonata in A Allegro Allegretto Allegro	CF	Classic Sonatas (Podolsky)
BACH, C. P. E. (1714-1788)	Allegro in A	P	Sonaten und Stücke
	Allegro in C		
	Allegro in E		
	Allegro in F Minor	Su	The Second Bach Book (Jonas)
	Allegro in G	P	Sonaten und Stücke
	Allegro in G	Sch C	Die Söhne Bach Eighteenth Century Music, Vol. II (No. 1)
	Allegro Siciliano	Su	The Second Bach Book (Jonas)
	Capriccio in D Minor (From Sonata 4)	Sch GS	Die Söhne Bach Introduction to Piano Classics, Vol. II (Mirovitch)
	La Capricieuse	U	Clavierstücke—C. P. E. Bach
	La Stahl	P	Sonaten und Stücke
	Presto in B-flat	Su	The Second Bach Book (Jonas)
	Presto in C Minor	Sch U U GS Su	Die Söhne Bach Old Masters for Young Pianists, Bk. 1 (Kuranda) Grosse Meister für Kleine Hände, Bk. 1 (Kuranda) Introduction to Piano Classics, Vol. II The Second Bach Book (Jonas)
	Rondo in B Minor	Su	The Second Bach Book (Jonas)
	Sonata in A Poco allegro Andante lusingando Allegro	Sch	Six Sonatas, Vol. I (No. 3)
	Sonata in C Minor Allegretto Molto adagio Allegro ma non tanto	P	Sonaten und Stücke

Composer	Title	Publisher	Volume or Collection

BACH, C. P. E. (cont.)	Sonata in D Minor
	    Allegro
	    Adagio sostenuto
	    Presto
		Sch	Six Sonatas, Vol. I (No. 2)

	Sonata in G Minor
	    Andante con amoroso
	    Allegretto
	    Allegro moderato
		P	Sonaten und Stücke

	Sonatina nuova in G	Sch	Die Söhne Bach
	Tempo di Minuetto	P	Sonaten und Stücke
	Twelve Variations auf die Folie d'Espagne		

	Gavotte in C Minor
	    (From Sonata 5, No. 6)
		H
		GS
		
		P
			The Sons of Bach
			Introduction to Piano Classics, Vol. II
			    (Mirovitch)
			Joh. Chr. Bach Sonatas, Bk. II

	Sonata in A, Op. XVII,
	    No. 5
	        Allegro
	        Presto
		P	Joh. Chr. Bach Sonatas, Bk. I

	Sonata in C Minor, Op. XVII,
	    No. 2
	        Allegro
	        Andante
	        Prestissimo		

	Sonata in D, Op. V,
	    No. 2
	        Allegro di molto
	        Andante di molto
	        Minuetto		

	Sonata in E, Op. V,
	    No. 5
	        Allegro
	        Andante
	        Allegro
		Sch
		P
			Die Söhne Bach
			Joh. Chr. Bach Sonatas, Bk. II

	Sonata in E-flat, Op. V,
	    No. 4
	        Allegro
	        Rondo
		P	Joh. Chr. Bach Sonatas, Bk. II

	Sonata in G, Op. XVII,
	    No. 4
	        Allegro
	        Presto assai
		P	Joh. Chr. Bach Sonatas, Bk. I

	Sonata in G, Op. V,
	    No. 3
	        Allegro
	        Allegretto		

	Theme and Variations, Op. V, No. 3	H P	The Sons of Bach Joh. Chr. Bach Sonatas, Bk. II

Composer	Title	Publisher	Volume or Collection
BACH, J. C. F. (1732-1795)	Allegretto (From Sonata in D)	Sch	Die Söhne Bach
	Andante (From Sonata in D)		
	Rondo (From Sonata in A)	H	The Sons of Bach
BACH, J. S. (1685-1750)	Air in E-flat (From French Suite in E-flat, No. IV)	K P GS	French Suites
	Air in E Minor (From Partita in E Minor, No. VI)	K P GS BMC	Partitas Bach for Early Grades, Bk. III
	Aria from Partita IV	ECS	Bach Verklärt
	Bourrée in A Minor (From English Suite in A Minor, No. II)	K P GS BMC PP MM Su	English Suites Bach for Early Grades, Bk. II Hundred Best Short Classics, Bk. III Your Bach Book (Maier) Bach Collection (Berlinger/Jonas)
	Bourée in E-flat	K	French Suites (pg. 64)
	Bourée in F	Sch Su	Little Bach Book (No. 5) Piano Literature of the 17th, 18th and 19th Centuries, Bk. 4a (Clark)
	Courante in A	B Sch	Hours with the Masters, Bk. II Little Piano Book of Wilhelm Friedemann (No. 12)
	Courante in E (From French Suite in E, No. VI)	K P GS	French Suites
	Courante in G (From Partita in G, No. v)	K P GS BMC	Partitas Bach for Early Grades, Bk. III
	Duet in E Minor	P K CF	Four Duets (No. 1) Road to Piano Artistry, Vol. IX (Scionti)
	Entrée in F	Sch	Little Bach Book (No. 2)
	Fuga in E-flat	K	Short Preludes and Fugues (pg. 48)
	Fughetta in D Minor	GS K GS P	Eighteen Little Preludes and Fugues (No. 6) Short Preludes and Fugues (pg. 41) Short Preludes and Fugues (pg. 27) Short Preludes and Fugues (pg. 36)
	Fughetta in E Minor	K GS	Short Preludes and Fugues (pg. 43) Short Preludes and Fugues (pg. 29)

Composer	Title	Publisher	Volume or Collection
BACH, J. S. (cont.)		P	Short Preludes and Fugues (pg. 40)
		GS	Eighteen Little Preludes and Fugues (No. 16)
	Fughetta in G	GS	Eighteen Little Preludes and Fugues (No. 3)
	Fugue in C	K	Short Preludes and Fugues (pg. 24)
		GS	Short Preludes and Fugues (pg. 22)
		P	Short Preludes and Fugues (pg. 30)
		GS	Eighteen Little Preludes and Fugues (No. 5)
	Fugue in C	K	Short Preludes and Fugues (pg. 26)
		GS	Short Preludes and Fugues (pg. 24)
		P	Short Preludes and Fugues (pg. 32)
		GS	Eighteen Little Preludes and Fugues (No. 13)
	Fugue in C Minor	K	Short Preludes and Fugues (pg. 22)
		GS	Eighteen Little Preludes and Fugues (No. 4)
		GS	Short Preludes and Fugues (pg. 20)
		P	Short Preludes and Fugues (pg. 28)
	Fugue in E Minor	K	Well Tempered Clavier, Bk. I
		P	
		GS	
		BMC	Bach for Early Grades, Bk. III
	Fugue in G	K	Well Tempered Clavier, Bk. II
		P	
		GS	
	Gavottes I and II (From English Suite in D Minor, No. VI)	K	English Suites
		P	
		GS	
	Gavotte (From French Suite in E, No. VI)	K	French Suites
		P	
		GS	
		Su	Bach Collection (Berlinger/Jonas)
		ECS	Bach Verklärt
	Gigue in A	Sch	Little Piano Book of Wilhelm Friedemann
		MM	Your Bach Book (Maier)
	Gigue in B-flat (From Partita in B-flat, No. I)	K	Partitas
		P	
		GS	
		GS	Bach Album (Heinze)
		PP	Hundred Best Short Classics, Bk. IV
		Su	Bach Collection (Berlinger/Jonas)
		ECS	Bach Verklärt
	Inventions--Two Part	K	Two Part Inventions
		P	
		GS	
		P	Inventionen und Sinfonien
		K	Bach's Little Notebook for Wilhelm Friedemann Bach

Composer	Title	Publisher	Volume or Collection
BACH, J. S. (cont.)	2. C Minor	MM	Your Bach Book (Maier)
	3. D Major		
	5. E-flat Major		
	6. E Major	ECS	Bach Verklärt
	10. G Major	ECS	Bach Verklärt
	11. G Minor		
	12. A Major		
	14. B-flat Major	MM	Your Bach Book (Maier)
		PP	Hundred Best Short Classics, Bk. II
	15. B Minor	MM	Your Bach Book (Maier)
	Inventions--Three Part	K	Three Part Inventions
		P	
		GS	
		P	Inventionen und Sinfonien
	1. C Major		
	2. C Minor		
	4. D Minor		
	5. E-flat Major		
	6. E Major	CF	Road to Piano Artistry, Vol. IX (Scionti)
	10. G Major	ECS	Bach Verklärt
	11. G Minor	CF	Road to Piano Artistry, Vol. VIII (Scionti)
	13. A Minor		
	15. B Minor		
	Little Prelude in A Minor	K	Short Preludes and Fugues (No. 12)
		GS	Eighteen Little Preludes and Fugues (No. 18)
		K	First Bach Book (No. 25)
		Sch	Little Bach Book (pg. 8)
		GS	Short Preludes and Fugues (No. 12)
	Little Prelude in D	K	Short Preludes and Fugues (pg. 8)
		GS	Short Preludes and Fugues (No. 4 of 12 Little)
		GS	Eighteen Little Preludes and Fugues (No. 13, Key of C)
		Sch	Little Piano Book of Wilhelm Friedemann (No. 15)
	Little Prelude in D (No. 4 from 6 Short Preludes)	K	Short Preludes and Fugues, (pg. 19)
		P	Short Preludes and Fugues, (pg. 22)
		GS	Eighteen Little Preludes and Fugues (No. 1)
		GS	Short Preludes and Fugues (pg. 17)
		PP	Hundred Best Short Classics, Bk. III
		CF	Road to Piano Artistry, Vol. VI (Scionti)
		WR	Rediscovered Classics, Bk. 3 (Henderson)
	Little Prelude in E	K	Short Preludes and Fugues (pg. 20)
		GS	Short Preludes and Fugues (pg. 18)
		U	Old Masters for Young Pianists (Kuranda), Bk. I
		P	Short Preludes and Fugues (pg. 24)
	Little Prelude in E Minor	K	Short Preludes and Fugues (pg. 21)
		GS	Short Preludes and Fugues (pg. 19)
		P	Short Preludes and Fugues (pg. 26)

Composer	Title	Publisher	Volume or Collection
BACH, J. S. (cont.)	Little Prelude in E Minor	K	Short Preludes and Fugues (pg. 42)
		GS	Short Preludes and Fugues (pg. 28)
		P	Short Preludes and Fugues (pg. 38)
	Little Prelude in F	K	Short Preludes and Fugues (pg. 12)
		GS	Short Preludes and Fugues (pg. 10)
		P	Short Preludes and Fugues (pg. 12)
		Sch	Little Piano Book of Wilhelm Friedemann (No. 16)
		K	Bach's Little Notebook for Wilhelm Friedemann Bach (No. 10)
	Little Prelude in F	GS	Eighteen Little Preludes and Fugues (No. 7)
	Little Prelude in G Minor	K	Short Preludes and Fugues (pg. 14)
		GS	Short Preludes and Fugues (pg. 12)
		P	Short Preludes and Fugues (pg. 14)
		K	First Bach Book (No. 24)
		Sch	Little Piano Book of Wilhelm Friedemann (No. 14)
	Little Prelude in G	GS	Eighteen Little Preludes and Fugues (No. 3)
	Minuet in B Minor, (From French Suite in B Minor, No. III)	K	French Suites
		P	
		GS	
		GS	Bach Album (Heinze)
		CF	
		BMC	Bach for Early Grades, Bk. III
		B	Hours With the Masters, Bk. III
		Su	Bach Collection (Berlinger/Jonas)
	Minuet in B-flat, (From Partita in B-flat, No. I)	K	Partitas
		P	
		GS	
		ECS	Bach Verklärt
		GS	Bach Album (Heinze)
		CF	
		Su	Bach Collection (Berlinger/Jonas)
	Minuets I and II in D Minor (From French Suite in D Minor No. I)	K	French Suites
		P	
		GS	
	Minuet in E Major (From French Suite VI)	K	French Suites
		P	
		GS	
		Su	Bach Collection (Berlinger/Jonas)
	Minuet in E-flat (From French Suite in E-flat No. IV)	K	French Suites
		P	
		GS	
	Minuets I and II in F (From English Suite in F No. IV)	K	English Suites
		P	
		GS	

Composer	Title	Publisher	Volume or Collection
BACH, J. S. (cont.)	Passepieds I and II (From English Suite in E Minor No. V)	K P GS GS CF ECS Su	English Suites Bach Album (Heinze) Bach Verklärt Bach Collection (Berlinger/Jonas)
	Polonaise in E (From French Suite in E No. VI)	K P GS GS BMC CF B U U	French Suites Master Series for the Young Bach for Early Grades, Bk. III Road to Piano Artistry, Vol. V (Scionti) Hours with the Masters, Bk. IV Old Masters for Young Pianists (Kuranda), Bk. I Grosse Meister für Kleine Hände, Bk. I
	Prelude in A-flat	K P GS	Well Tempered Clavier, Vol. I
	Prelude in A Minor		(No. 22)
	Prelude in B-flat		(No. 21)
	Prelude in B		(No. 23)
	Prelude in B Minor	K P GS	Well Tempered Clavier, Vol. II (No. 24)
	Prelude in C Minor	P K GS K	Well Tempered Clavier, Vol. I (No. 2) Bach's Little Notebook for Wilhelm Friedemann Bach (No. 15)
	Prelude in D Minor	K P GS K	Well Tempered Clavier, Vol. I (No. 6) Bach's Little Notebook for Wilhelm Friedemann Bach (No. 16)
	Prelude in E-flat	K P GS	Well Tempered Clavier, Vol. II (No. 7)
	Prelude in F Minor	 K ECS	(No. 12) Little Notebook for Wilhelm Friedemann Bach (No. 26) Bach Verklärt
	Prelude in F Minor	GS CF Sch	First Lessons in Bach, Bk. II (Carroll) Bach First Lessons, Bk. II (Carroll) Little Bach Book
	Prelude in G	K P GS	Well Tempered Clavier, Vol. I (No. 15)

Composer	Title	Publisher	Volume or Collection
BACH, J. S. (cont.)	Prelude in G	K P GS	Well Tempered Clavier, Vol. II (No. 15)
	Sarabande in A Minor (From English Suite in A Minor No. II)	K P GS MM ECS	English Suites Your Bach Book (Maier) Bach Verklärt
	Sarabande in D Minor (From French Suite in D Minor No. I)	K P GS GS CF B	French Suites Bach Album (Heinze) Hours with the Masters, Bk. V
	Sarabande in E-flat (From French Suite in E-flat No. IV)	K P GS ECS	French Suites Bach Verklärt
	Sarabande in E Minor (From English Suite In E Minor No. V)	K P GS GS CF CF GS PP ECS	English Suites Bach Album (Heinze) Bach First Lessons, Bk. II First Lessons in Bach, Bk. II Hundred Best Classics, Bk. III Bach Verklärt
	Sarabande in F (From English Suite in F No. IV)	K P GS	English Suites
	Sarabande in F Minor	Sch	Little Bach Book
	Sarabande in G Minor (From English Suite in G Minor No. III)	K P GS	English Suites
	Scherzo in A Minor (From Partita in A Minor)	K P GS CF Su ECS	Partitas Bach First Lessons, Bk. II Bach Collection (Berlinger/Jonas) Bach Verklärt
	Solo per il Cembalo	K P	Little Notebook of Anna Magdalena Bach Notenbuch der Anna Magdalena Bach (Sauer)
	Tempo di Menuetto (From Partita V)	ECS	Bach Verklärt
BACH, W. F. (1710-1784)	Fuga in B-flat (Fughetta)	P GS	Fugues and Polonaises (No. 7) Eighteen Little Preludes and Fugues (No. 5)

Composer	Title	Publisher	Volume or Collection
BACH, W. F. (cont.)	Fuga in D	P Sch	Fugues and Polonaises (No. 3) Die Söhne Bach
	(Fughetta)	GS	Eighteen Little Preludes and Fugues (No. 1)
	Fuga in D Minor (Fughetta)	P GS	Fugues and Polonaises (No. 4) Eighteen Little Preludes and Fugues (No. 2)
	Lamento in E Minor	Sch GS	Die Söhne Bach Introduction to Piano Classics, Vol. II (Mirovitch)
	(Sarabande from Sonata in G)	H	The Sons of Bach
	Polonaise in C Minor	P H	Fugues and Polonaises (No. 2) The Sons of Bach
	Polonaise in D Minor	P Sch	Fugues and Polonaises (No. 4) Die Söhne Bach
	Polonaise in F	P Sch	Fugues and Polonaises (No. 9) Die Söhne Bach
BLOW, J. (1649-1708)	Courante and Fugue in C	GS A	Early Keyboard Music, Vol. I Beringer's School of Easy Classics: Old English and French Masters
	Prelude in C	GS	Early Keyboard Music, Vol. I
BÖHM, G. (1661-1733)	Presto in G Minor	K	Old Masters of the 16th, 17th and 18th Centuries
BULL, J. (1563-1628)	Courante, Jewell	GS	Early Keyboard Music, Vol. I
	Galiardo II in D Minor		
BYRD, W. (1542-1623)	Galiardo in G Minor	GS	Early Keyboard Music, Vol. I
	Sellenger's Round		
	The Carman's Whistle		
	Victoria		
CIMAROSA, D. (1749-1801)	Sonatas: Nos. 1, 3, 4, 6, 7, 8, 10	E BB	Thirty Two Sonatas, Vol. I
	Sonatas: Nos. 11, 12, 14, 18, 19, 20		Thirty Two Sonatas, Vol. II
	Sonatas: (12 Sonatas) Complete		Thirty Two Sonatas, Vol. III
CORELLI, A. (1653-1713)	Giga	PP K	Hundred Best Short Classics, Bk. IV Corelli, 24 Pieces For The Piano, Vol. I
COUPERIN, F. (1668-1733)	Gavotte in G Minor	BH	Airs and Dances, Bk. II (Dorolle)
	La Bandoline--Rondeau	GS	Early Keyboard Music, Vol. II
	Les Petits Moulins á Vent	K	Old Masters of the 16th, 17th and 18th Centuries

Composer	Title	Publisher	Volume or Collection
COUPERIN, F. (cont.)		He	A Treasury of Easy Classics (Abrams)
		GS	Early Keyboard Music, Vol. II
		A	Beringer's School of Easy Classics: Old English and French Masters
		GS	Published Separately
		B	Hours With The Masters, Bk. 4
	Rigaudon in D Minor	K	Old Masters of the 16th, 17th and 18th Centuries
	Rondeau	K	Little Notebook of Anna Magdalena Bach
	Soeuer Monique	GS	Early Keyboard Music, Vol. II
		GS	Published Separately
		PP	Hundred Best Short Classics, Bk. V
	Chaconne in D Minor	GS	Early Keyboard Music, Vol. I
DAQUIN (1694-1772)	Le Coucou	K	Old Masters of the 16th, 17th and 18th Centuries
		B	Hours with the Masters, Bk. V
		PP	Hundred Best Short Classics, Bk. III
FISCHER, J. K. F. (1650-1746)	Fugue in G	K	A Little Book of Fugues (No. 10)
	Prelude (From Second Suite)	K	Old Masters of the 16th, 17th and 18th Centuries
	Rondeau (From Second Suite)			
	Sarabande in D Minor			
GALUPPI, B. (1706-1785)	Adagio (From Sonata in D)	K	Old Masters of the 16th, 17th and 18th Centuries
		CF	Classic Sonatas (Podolsky)
		OD	Early Italian Piano Music
		WR	Rediscovered Classics, Bk. 4 (Henderson)
	Vivace in C Minor	HC	Clavecinistes Italiens
GIBBONS, O. (1583-1675)	The Queen's Command	GS	Early Keyboard Music, Vol. I
GRAUN, C. H. (1701-1759)	Gigue in B-flat Minor	K	Old Masters of the 16th, 17th and 18th Centuries
GRAZIOLI, G. (1770-1820)	Sonata in G	CF	Published Separately
		Ho	
	Moderato		
	Adagio		
	Tempo di Minuetto		
	Singing to the Lute (From Sonata in G)	SG	Classics from the 17th and 18th Centuries
	Minuetto in G (From Sonata in G)	OD	Early Italian Piano Music

Composer	Title	Publisher	Volume or Collection
HANDEL, G. F. (1685-1759)	Air in G (From Suite XIV)	K	Suites and Chaconnes, Vol. II
		P	Handel Suites, Vol. II
		GS	Master Series for the Young
		GS	Twelve Easy Pieces
		He	A Little Treasury of Classics, Bk. IV
	(Allegro)	U	Old Masters for Young Pianists (Kuranda)
	Air and Variations in B-flat	K	Suites and Chaconnes, Vol. II
	Air and Variations in E (From Suite V)	K	Suites and Chaconnes, Vol. I
		P	Suites, Vol. I
	(Harmonious Blacksmith)	PP	Hundred Best Short Classics, Bk. IV
		GS	Master Series for the Young
	Air and Variations in F	Sch	Aylesford Pieces No. 16
		Sch	Pieces for Harpsichord, Vol. II (No. 53)
	Allegro in D Minor (From Suite X)	K	Suites and Chaconnes, Vol. II
		P	Suites, Vol. II
	Allegro in D Minor	Sch	Aylesford Pieces (No. 11)
		Sch	Pieces for Harpsichord, Vol. II (No. 54)
	Allegro I in F (From Suite II)	K	Suites and Chaconnes, Vol. I
		P	Suites, Vol. I
	Allegro in G (From Suite XIV)	K	Suites, Vol. II
		P	Suites, Vol. II
		PP	Hundred Best Short Classics, Bk. V
	Allegro in G Minor (From Suite VII)	K	Suites, Vol. I
		P	Suites, Vol. I
		H	Easiest Original Pieces
	Allemande in A Minor	Sch	Pieces for Harpsichord, Vol. II (No. 43)
		Sch	Aylesford Pieces (No. 17)
	Allemande in F Minor (From Suite VIII)	K	Suites, Vol. I
		P	Suites, Vol. I
		GS	Twelve Easy Pieces
		GS	Master Series for the Young
	Allemande in G (From Suite XIV)	K	Suites, Vol. II
		P	Suites, Vol. II
		H	Easiest Original Pieces (No. 6)
	Allemande in G Minor (From Suite XVI)	P	Suites, Vol. II
		GS	Twelve Easy Pieces
		GS	Master Series for the Young
		B	Hours with the Masters, Bk. V
	Aria in C Minor	Sch	Pieces for Harpsichord, Vol. I (No. 13)
	Aria in C Minor	Sch	Pieces for Harpsichord, Vol. II (No. 52)
	Arpeggio and Gigue in G Minor	Sch	Pieces for Harpsichord, Vol. I (Nos. 19 and 20)
	Capriccio in A Minor	GS	Master Series for the Young
	(Fantasie in A Minor)	PP	Hundred Best Short Classics, Bk. IV
	Chaconne in C	Sch	Pieces for Harpsichord, Vol. I (No. 15)

Composer	Title	Publisher	Volume or Collection
HANDEL, G. F. (cont.)	Chaconne in G No. 2	K	Suites, Vol. II
	Chaconne in G, No. 9	K	Suites, Vol. II
	Chaconne in G Minor	Sch	Pieces for Harpsichord, Vol. II (No. 45)
	Concerto	Sch	Pieces for Harpsichord, Vol. I (No. 33)
		Sch	Aylesford Pieces (No. 7)
	Courante in F Minor (From Suite VIII)	K	Suites, Vol. I
		P	Suites, Vol. I
	Courante in G (From Suite XIV)	K	Suites, Vol. II
		P	Suites, Vol. II
		H	Easiest Original Pieces
		GS	Master Series for the Young
	(Corrente)	GS	Twelve Easy Pieces
	Entrée	Sch	Pieces for Harpsichord, Vol. I (No. 2)
		Sch	Aylesford Pieces (No. 2)
	Fantasia in C	H	Easiest Original Pieces
		B	Hours with the Masters, Bk. V
	(Sonata in C)	CF	Classic Sonatas (Podolsky)
	(Sonata in C)	GS	Twelve Easy Pieces
	Fughetta in D (From Six Fughettas)	H	Easiest Original Pieces
	Gavotte and Variations in G (From Suite XIV)	P	Suites, Vol. II
		K	Suites, Vol. II
		GS	Master Series for the Young (Incomplete)
		GS	Twelve Easy Pieces
	Gigue in B-flat (From Suite XIII)	K	Suites, Vol. II
		P	Suites, Vol. II
		H	Easiest Original Pieces
	Gigue in D Minor (From Suite XI)	K	Suites, Vol. II
		P	Suites, Vol. II
		GS	Master Series for the Young
		GS	Twelve Easy Pieces
	Gigue in G Major (From Suite XIV)	K	Suites, Vol. II
		P	Suites, Vol. II
		GS	Master Series for the Young
	Gigue in G Minor (From Suite XVI)	K	Suites, Vol. II
		P	Suites, Vol. II
		B	Hours with the Masters, Bk. III
	Little Fugue No. 2 in C	GS	Master Series for the Young
	Menuet in A Minor	Sch	Pieces for Harpsichord, Vol. II (No. 68)
	Menuet in D Minor	Sch	Pieces for Harpsichord, Vol. II (No. 55)
	Menuetto in D Minor (From Suite X)	K	Suites, Vol. II
		P	Suites, Vol. II
	Ouverture in G Minor	Sch	Pieces for Harpsichord, Vol. I (No. 1)
		Sch	Aylesford Pieces (No. 1)

Composer	Title	Publisher	Volume or Collection
HANDEL, G. F. (cont.)	Passacaglia in G Minor (From Suite VII)	K P GS	Suites, Vol. I Suites, Vol. I Master Series for the Young
	Prelude in A Minor	Sch	Pieces for Harpsichord, Vol. I (No. 17)
	Prelude in C	Sch	Pieces for Harpsichord, Vol. I (No. 12)
	Prelude in D Minor	Sch	Pieces for Harpsichord, Vol. II (No. 49)
	Prelude in D Minor	Sch Sch	Pieces for Harpsichord, Vol. I (No. 10) Aylesford Pieces (No. 8)
	Sonata in G Minor	Sch	Pieces for Harpsichord, Vol. I (No. 31)
	Sonata in G Minor	Sch	(No. 32)
	Sonatina in A Minor	Sch Sch	Pieces for Harpsichord, Vol. II (No. 44) Aylesford Pieces (No. 20)
	Suite in B-flat, No. XIII Allemande Courante Sarabande Gigue	K P	Suites, Vol. II Suites, Vol. II
	Suite in D Minor, No. XI Allemande Courante Sarabande Gigue	K P	Suites, Vol. II Suites, Vol. II
	Suite in D Minor, No. XV Allemande Courante Sarabande Gigue	P K	Suites, Vol. II
	Suite in E, No. V Prelude Allemande Courante Air and Variations	P K	Suites, Vol. I
	Suite in E Minor, No. XII Allemande Sarabande Gigue	P K	Suites, Vol. II
	Suite in G, No. XIV Allemande Allegro Courante Air Menuet Gavotte and Variations	K P	Suites, Vol. II Suites, Vol. II

Composer	Title	Publisher	Volume or Collection
HANDEL, G. F. (cont.)	Suite in G Minor, No. VII Ouverture Andante Allegro Sarabande Gigue Passacaille	K P	Suites, Vol. I Suites, Vol. II
	Suite in G Minor, No. XVI Allemande Courante Sarabande Gigue	P	Suites, Vol. II
HASSE, J. A. (1699-1783)	Adagio in D Minor (From Sonata Op. 7)	GS	Introduction to Piano Classics, Vol. III (Mirovitch)
	Allegro, Op. 7, No. 6	GS	Early Classics for the Piano (Mirovitch)
	Allegro in B-flat	CF GS	Classic Sonatas (Podolsky) Introduction to Piano Classics, Vol. III
	Gigue in D Minor (From Sonata Op. 7)	GS CF GS	Introduction to Piano Classics, Vol. III Classic Sonatas (Podolsky) Early Classics for the Piano (Mirovitch)
HÄSSLER, J. W. (1747-1822)	Sonata in C (From Six Easy Sonatas), No. I Poco Allegro Largo Allegro quasi presto	CF P	Classic Sonatas (Podolsky) Six Easy Sonatas
	Sonata in C (From Six Easy Sonatas), No. II Largo ed espressivo Allegro molto	CF P	Classic Sonatas (Podolsky) Six Easy Sonatas
HAYDN, J. (1732-1809)	Adagio (From Sonata in G)	P K U H	Haydn Sonatas, Vol. IV (No. 37) Vol. II (No. 31) Haydn Sonatas, Vol. III (No. 22) Easiest Original Pieces
	Allegro molto (From Sonata in G)	P K U	Haydn Sonatas, Vol. IV (No. 37) Vol. II (No. 31) Vol. III (No. 22)
	Andante (From Sonata in D)	P K GS U	Haydn Sonatas, Vol. I (No. 9) Vol. Ia (No. 9) Vol. I (No. 9) Vol. II (No. 16)
	Arietta con Variazione in A Major	K A P	Haydn: Eight Various Compositions Beringer's School of Easy Classics: Haydn Haydn: Piano Pieces
	Arietta con Variazione in E-flat	K H P	Haydn: Eight Various Compositions Easiest Original Pieces Haydn: Piano Pieces

Composer	Title	Publisher	Volume or Collection
HAYDN, J. (cont.)	Finale: Allegro assai (From Sonata in D)	P K GS U	Haydn: Sonatas, Vol. I (No. 9) Vol. Ia (No. 9) Vol. I (No. 9) Vol. I (No. 16)
	Finale: Presto (From Sonata in A)	P H	Haydn Sonatas, Vol. III (No. 33) Easiest Original Pieces
	Finale: Presto (From Sonata in D)	P H	Haydn Sonatas, Vol. III (No. 31) Easiest Original Pieces
	Finale: Tempo di Menuetto (From Sonata in E-flat)	P K GS U	Haydn Sonatas, Vol. I (No. 3) Vol. Ia (No. 3) Vol. I (No. 3) Vol. III (No. 25)
	Finale: Tempo di Menuetto (From Sonata in E)	P K U	Haydn Sonatas, Vol. IV (No. 40) Vol. II (No. 34) Vol. II (No. 19)
	Menuetto (From Sonata in G)	P K U	Haydn Sonatas, Vol. IV (No. 37) Vol. II (No. 31) Vol. III (No. 22)
	Rondo in A	GS	Published Separately

	Sonata in A
	  Allegro
	  Menuetto
	  Presto
		P	Haydn Sonatas, Vol. II (No. 23)

	Sonata in A
	  Andante
	  Menuetto
	  Finale
		P
		K
		U
		R
			Haydn Sonatas, Vol. III (No. 29)
			Vol. II (No. 26)
			Vol. I (No. 5)
			Haydn-Mozart, Easy Composition

	Sonata in A
	  Allegro
	  Adagio
	  Tempo di Menuetto con
	    variazioni
		P
		K
		U
			Haydn Sonatas, Vol. IV (No. 36)
			Vol. II (No. 30)
			Vol. I (No. 6)

	Sonata in A-flat
	  Moderato
	  Menuetto
	  Rondo
		P	Vol. IV (No. 41)

	Sonata in B-flat
	  Moderato
	  Largo
	  Menuetto
		P	Vol. II (No. 22)

	Sonata in C
	  Allegro con brio
	  Adagio
	  Finale
		P
		K
		GS
		U
		P
			Vol. I (No. 5)
			Vol. Ia (No. 5)
			Vol. I (No. 5)
			Vol. I (No. 2)
			Sonaten Album, Vol. I

	Sonata in D
	  Allegro con brio
	  Largo e sostenuto
		P
		K
		GS
			Vol. I (No. 7)
			Vol. Ia (No. 7)
			Vol. I (No. 7)

Composer	Title	Publisher	Volume or Collection
HAYDN, J. (cont.)	Finale	U	Vol. II (No. 17)
		P	Sonaten Album, Vol. I
	Sonata in D	P	Vol. II (No. 20)
	Allegro	K	Vol. Ib (No. 19)
	Adagio	GS	Vol. II (No. 19)
	Tempo di Menuetto	U	Vol. II (No. 11)
	Sonata in E	P	Vol. II (No. 18)
	Moderato	K	Vol. Ib (No. 17)
	Menuetto	GS	Vol. II (No. 17)
	Finale	U	Vol. I (No. 4)
		R	Haydn-Mozart, Easy Compositions
	Sonata in E Minor	P	Vol. I (No. 2)
	Presto	K	Vol. Ia (No. 2)
	Adagio	GS	Vol. I (No. 2)
	Finale	U	Vol. II (No. 14)
		P	Sonaten Album, Vol. I
	Sonata in F	P	Vol. II (No. 21)
	Allegro moderato	K	Vol. Ib (No. 20)
	Adagio	GS	Vol. II (No. 20)
	Finale	U	Vol. I (No. 10)
	Sonata in F	P	Vol. IV (No. 34)
	Moderato	K	Vol. II (No. 28)
	Larghetto	U	Vol. I (No. 7)
	Allegro		
	Sonata in G	P	Vol. II (No. 12)
	Allegro con brio	GS	Vol. II (No. 11)
	Menuetto	K	Vol. Ib (No. 11)
	Finale	U	Vol. I (No. 1)
		GS	Master Series for the Young
		P	Sonaten Album, Vol. I
	Sonata in G	P	Vol. II (No. 17)
	Allegro con brio	K	Vol. Ib (No. 16)
	Adagio	GS	Vol. II (No. 16)
	Prestissimo	U	Vol. III (No. 24)
	Tema con Variazioni	K	Eight Various Compositions
		GS	Master Series for the Young
		P	Haydn, Klavierstücke
KIRNBERGER, J. (1721-1783)	Gigue in C Minor	K	Old Masters of the 16th, 17th and 18th Centuries (pg. 39)
	Gavotte in D Minor		(pg. 38)
KRIEGER, J. (1649-1725)	Corrente	K	Old Masters of the 16th, 17th and 18th Centuries
	Sarabande with Double		
KUHNAU, J. (1660-1722)	Bourrée in D Minor	K	Old Masters of the 16th, 17th and 18th Centuries
	Gigue in C Minor		

Composer	Title	Publisher	Volume or Collection
KUHNAU, J. (cont.)	Prelude in B Minor	EV	New Recital Repertoire (Mirovitch)
LOEILLET, J. (1653-1728)	Suite in G Minor Allemande Courante Sarabande Minuetto Gigue	GS	Early Keyboard Music, Bk. II
LULLY, J. B. (1632-1687)	Courante in E Minor	GS	Early Keyboard Music, Bk. I
	Sarabande in C		
MARPURG, F. W. (1718-1795)	La Badine	K	Old Masters of the 16th, 17th and 18th Centuries
	La Voltigeuse		
MATTHESON, J. (1681-1764)	Air (From C Minor, Suite No. 5) (Aria)	GS BH	Early Keyboard Music, Bk. II Airs and Dances, Bk. II (Dorolle)
	Gigue in E Minor	GS K GS	Early Keyboard Music, Bk. II Old Masters of the 16th, 17th and 18th Centuries Introduction to Piano Classics, Bk. III (Mirovitch)
	Gigue II in G Minor	GS	Early Keyboard Music, Bk. II
	Sarabande mit Drei Variations (From Suite XII)	GS	Early Keyboard Music, Bk. II
MEHUL, E. (1763-1817)	Sonata in A, Op. 1, No. 3	CF	Published Separately (Podolsky)
MOZART, W. A. (1756-1791)	Adagio (K 540)	P P	Mozart: Klavierstücke (Urtext) Mozart: Selected Piano Pieces (Urtext)
	Adagio (From Sonata in F) (K 280)	K P	Mozart Sonatas and Three Fantasies Mozart Sonatas
	Ah! Vous Dirai-je Maman (Complete) (From Variations)	R H GS P	Haydn-Mozart, Easy Compositions Easiest Original Pieces Master Series for the Young Sonatinen Vorstüfe, Vol. I
	Fantasie in D Minor (K 397)	K GS GS P P R A Wo	Mozart Fantasies, K 396 and 397 Mozart—Twelve Piano Pieces Mozart Fantasias and Rondos Mozart: Klavierstücke (Urtext) Mozart: Selected Piano Pieces (Urtext) Haydn-Mozart, Easy Compositions Published Separately Published Separately
	Menuetto in D (K 355)	K GS	Mozart, Various Pieces Mozart, Twelve Piano Pieces

Composer	Title	Publisher	Volume or Collection
MOZART, W. A. (cont.)		GS	Master Series for the Young
		P	Mozart: Selected Piano Pieces (Urtext)
		P	Mozart: Klavierstücke (Urtext)
	Rondo in D (K 485)	K	Mozart, Various Pieces
		GS	Mozart, Twelve Piano Pieces
		GS	Mozart Fantasias and Rondos
		H	Easiest Original Pieces
		GS	Master Series for the Young
		P	Mozart: Klavierstücke (Urtext)
		P	Mozart: Selected Piano Pieces (Urtext)
		R	Haydn-Mozart, Easy Compositions
		P	Sonatinen Album, Vol. I
	Rondo in F (K 494)	K	Mozart Various Pieces
		P	Mozart: Selected Piano Pieces (Urtext)
	Sonata in A (K 331)	K	Mozart Sonatas
	Andante grazioso	P	
	Menuetto	P	Sonaten Album, Vol. I
	Alla Turca		
	Sonata in G (K 283)	K	Mozart Sonatas
	Allegro	P	
	Andante	P	Sonaten Album, Vol. I
	Presto		
	Sonatina in A, No. II	Sch	Six Viennese Sonatinas
	Allegro	H	
	Menuetto	MMC	
	Adagio	I	
	Rondo	P	
		He	
		GS	
	Sonatina in B-flat, No. IV	Sch	Six Viennese Sonatinas
	Andante grazioso	H	
	Menuetto	MMC	
	Rondo	I	
		P	
		He	
		GS	
	Sonatina in C, No. I	Sch	Six Viennese Sonatinas
	Allegro brilliante	H	
	Allegretto	MMC	
	Adagio	I	
	Allegro	P	
		He	
		GS	
	Sonatina in C, No. VI	Sch	Six Viennese Sonatinas
	Allegro	H	
	Menuetto	MMC	
	Adagio	I	
	Finale	P	
		He	
		GS	
		CF	Road to Piano Artistry, Vol. VIII (Scionti)

Composer	Title	Publisher	Volume or Collection
MOZART, W. A. (cont.)	Sonatina in D, No. III	Sch	Six Viennese Sonatinas
	Andante	H	
	Menuetto	MMC	
	Rondo	I	
		P	
		He	
		GS	
MUFFAT, J. T. (1690-1770)	Allegro spiritoso	GS	Early Keyboard Music, Vol. II
	Fantasia in G Minor	GS	Introduction to Piano Classics, Vol. III (Mirovitch)
	Fugues, Nos. 6, 7, 8, 11, 15, 17	K	A Little Book of Fugues
	Menuet in D Minor	K	Old Masters of the 16th, 17th and 18th Centuries
	Partita in C	Sch	Partiten und Stücke
	Prelude		
	Fantasie		
	Sarabanda		
	Rigaudon		
	Menuet		
	Paysan		
	Partita in C Minor	Sch	Partiten und Stücke
	Ouverture		
	Allemande		
	Courante		
	Sarabande		
	Gavotte		
	Menuet		
	Gigue		
	Rigaudon in F	K	Old Masters of the 16th, 17th and 18th Centuries
	Suite in B-flat	GS	Early Keyboard Music, Bk. II
	Sarabande		
	La Hardiesse		
	Minuet I		
	Minuet II		
	Air		
	Gigue		
	Zwei kleine Fugen	Sch	Partiten und Stücke
MURCHHAUSER, F. (1663-1738)	Aria Pastoralis Variata	K	Old Masters of the 16th, 17th and 18th Centuries
		GS	Early Keyboard Music, Bk. II
	Fugue in F	K	A Little Book of Fugues (No. 13)
NEEFE, C. G. (1748-1798)	Toccata	GS	Introduction to Piano Classics, Vol. III (Mirovitch)

Composer	Title	Publisher	Volume or Collection
NICHELMANN, C. (1717-1762)	Gigue in C Minor	K	Old Masters of the 16th, 17th and 18th Centuries
	La Galliarde in C		
	La Tendre		
PACHELBEL, J. (1653-1706)	Ciaconna in D	GS	Early Keyboard Music, Bk. I
	Fugue in C Minor	EV	New Recital Repertoire (Mirovitch)
	Fugue in D Minor	K	A Little Book of Fugues (No. 12)
	Fugue in F	K	(No. 16)
		K	Old Masters of the 16th, 17th and 18th Centuries
		EV	New Recital Repertoire (Mirovitch)
	Fugues on the Magnificat, Nos. 4, 5, 6	K	Old Masters of the 16th, 17th and 18th Centuries
PARADISI, D. (1710-1792)	Toccata in D Minor	GS	Early Classics for the Piano (Mirovitch)
PURCELL, H. (1658-1695)	Prelude in C (From Suite in C, No. V)	GS	Purcell Keyboard Suites
		GS	Early Keyboard Music, Bk. I
		B	Hours with the Masters, Bk. IV
		GS	Introduction to Piano Classics, Vol. III (Mirovitch)
		H	Contemporaries of Purcell
	Suite in A Minor, No. IV	GS	Purcell: Keyboard Suites
		GS	Early Keyboard Music, Bk. I
	Prelude		
	Almand		
	Courante		
	Sarabande		
	Suite in C, No. V		
	Prelude		
	Almand		
	Courante		
	Saraband		
	Cebell (Gavot)		
	Minuet		
	Riggadoon		
	Intrada		
	March		
	Suite in D, No. VI		
	Prelude		
	Almand		
	Hornpipe		
	Suite in D Minor, No. VII		
	Almand		
	Courante		
	Hornpipe		

Composer	Title	Publisher	Volume or Collection

PURCELL, H. (cont.)	Suite in F, No. VIII
	  Prelude
	  Almand
	  Hornpipe
	  Minuet		

RAMEAU, J. P. (1683-1764)	Gigue en Rondeau in E Minor	GS	Early Keyboard Music, Bk. II
	Gigue en Rondeau in E	BH	Airs and Dances, Bk. II (Dorolle)
	Musette en Rondeau	K	Old Masters of the 16th, 17th and 18th Centuries
		A	Beringer's School of Easy Classics: Old English and French Masters
		GS	Early Keyboard Music, Bk. II
	Rigaudon in E, II	GS	Early Keyboard Music, Bk. II
RUTINI, G. M. (1730-1797)	Giga	HC	Clavecinistes Italiens
	Presto in F Minor		
SCARLATTI, A. (1659-1725)	Tema con Variazioni in E-flat	OD	Early Italian Piano Music
	(Toccata Settima)	K	Easy Pieces From Old Italian Masters
SCARLATTI, D. (1685-1757)	Larghetto in F	GS	Early Keyboard Music, Bk. II
	Siciliano in F	K	Old Masters of the 16th, 17th and 18th Centuries
		A	Beringer's School of Easy Classics: Scarlatti (No. 5)
	Sonata in A, L. 94	M	Twelve Easy Scarlatti Sonatas (Mirovitch) (No. 8)
	Sonat in A Minor, L. 93		(No. 7)
	Sonata in B Minor, L. 263	CF	Road to Piano Artistry, Vol. VII (Scionti)
		K	Sixty Sonatas
		R	Twenty Five Sonatas
		BMC	Twenty Seven Selected Sonatas
	Sonata in C, (L 358)	M	Twelve Easy Scarlatti Sonatas (Mirovitch) (No. 10)
		GS	Early Keyboard Music, Bk. II
	Sonata in D, (L 463)	P	Twenty Five Sonatas
		I	9 Sonatas
		GS	Early Keyboard Music, Bk. II
		PP	Hundred Best Short Classics, Bk. V
		OD	Early Italian Piano Music
		K	Sixty Sonatas
		R	Twenty Five Sonatas
		A	Beringer's School of Easy Classics: Scarlatti
	Sonata in D Minor, (L 413) (Pastorale)	M	Twelve Easy Scarlatti Sonatas (Mirovitch) (No. 11)

Composer	Title	Publisher	Volume or Collection
SCARLATTI, D. (cont.)	(Pastorale)	P	Twenty Five Sonatas
		GS	Early Keyboard Music, Bk. II
		K	Sixty Sonatas
		PP	Hundred Best Short Classics, Bk. V
		A	Beringer's School of Easy Classics: Scarlatti
	(Pastorale in E Minor)	I	9 Sonatas for Piano
		CF	Road to Piano Artistry, Vol. IV (Scionti)
	Sonata in F, (L 433) (Siciliano)	OD	Early Italian Piano Music
		K	Old Masters of the 16th, 17th and 18th Centuries
	(Pastorale)	K	Sixty Sonatas (No. 43)
		R	Twenty Five Sonatas (No. 17)
	Sonata in G, (L 388)	M	Twelve Easy Scarlatti Sonatas (Mirovitch) (No. 9)
		K	Sixty Sonatas (No. 2)
	Sonata in G Minor, (L 386)	M	Twelve Easy Scarlatti Sonatas
SOLER, A. (1724-1783)	Sonata in A Minor	Su	Portuguese and Spanish Keyboard Music
	Sonata in D Major		
	Sonata in D Minor		
SPETH, J. (?)	Fugue in D Minor	K	A Little Book of Fugues (No. 5)
TELEMANN, G. P. (1681-1767)	Fantasia in B-flat	EV	New Recital Repertoire (Mirovitch)
	Fantasia in F, No. II	GS	Introduction to Piano Classics, Vol. III (Mirovitch)
		Sch	Telemann: Kleine Fantasien (No. 5)
	Fantasia in G Minor, No. I	GS	Introduction to Piano Classics, Vol. III (Mirovitch)
		Sch	Telemann: Kleine Fantasien (No. 6)
	Fantasia in G Minor, No. III	GS	Introduction to Piano Classics, Vol. III (Mirovitch)
	Seven Fantasies	Sch	Kleine Fantasien
TURINI, F. (1749-1812)	Molto allegro	HC	Clavecinistes Italiens
		OD	Early Italian Piano Music
	Presto in G Minor	HC	Clavecinistes Italiens
ZIPOLI, D. (1675-1726)	Gavotta in B Minor	K	Old Masters of the 16th, 17th and 18th Centuries
	Suite in B Minor Preludio	OD	Early Italian Piano Music
	Corrente Aria Gavotta	GS	Early Classics for the Piano (Mirovitch)

Composer	Title	Publisher	Volume or Collection
ALBÉNIZ, I. (1860-1909)	Córdoba, Op. 232, No. 4	UME I Ho GS	Chants d'Espagne Cantos de Espana Published Separately
	Granada	UME I M	Suite Espanole No. I Published Separately
	Malaguena	M	Published Separately
	Orientale, Op. 232, No. 2	UME I	Chants d'Espagne Cantos de Espana
	Seguidillas, Op. 232, No. 5	UME M I	Chants d'Espagne Published Separately Cantos de Espana
	Sevilla	UME I M	Suite Espagnole Published Separately
	Tango in D	BMC	Published Separately
	Tango, Op. 164, No. 2	GS	51 Piano Pieces from the Modern Repertoire
ALBENIZ, M. (1760-1831)	Sonata in D Major	Su	Portuguese and Spanish Keyboard Music
BEETHOVEN, L. van (1770-1827)	Adagio, (From Sonata Op. 2, No. 1)	K P SS ABR	Beethoven Sonatas, Vol. I (Donald Tovey ed.)
	Adagio cantabile, (From Sonata. Op. 13)		
	Adagio sostenuto, (From Sonata, Op. 27, No. 2)		
	Allegretto, (From Sonata Op. 27, No. 2)		
	Allegro, (From Sonata, Op. 2, No. 1)		
	Allegro molto e con brio, (From Sonata, Op. 10, No. 1)		
	Andante (From Sonata, Op. 14, No. 2)	K P SS ABR	Beethoven Sonatas, Vol. I (Donald Tovey ed.)

Composer	Title	Publisher	Volume or Collection
BEETHOVEN,		B	Hours with the Masters, Bk. V
L. van		GS	Master Series for the Young
(cont.)			
	Andante, (From Sonata, Op. 79)	K	Beethoven Sonatas, Vol. II
		P	
		SS	
		GS	Master Series for the Young
	Bagatelles, Op. 33 (Complete)	GS	Bagatelles, Op. 33
		P	Various Pieces
		K	Various Pieces
		GS	Beethoven Easy Compositions
	Bagatelle in B-flat, Op. 119, No. 11	I	Bagatelles, Op. 119
		P	Various Pieces
		K	Various Pieces
		GS	Beethoven, Easy Compositions
		K	Easy Compositions by Mozart and Beethoven
		GS	Master Series for the Young
	Bagatelle in C, Op. 119, No. 2	I	Bagatelles, Op. 119
		P	Various Pieces
		K	Various Pieces
		H	Easiest Original Pieces
	Bagatelle in C, Op. 119, No. 7	I	Bagatelles, Op. 119
		P	Various Pieces
		K	Various Pieces
		GS	Thirty-two Sonatinas and Rondos
	Bagatelle in C, Op. 119, No. 8	I	Bagatelles, Op. 119
		P	Various Pieces
		K	Various Pieces
	Bagatelle in C Minor, Op. 119, No. 5	I	Bagatelles, Op. 119
		P	Various Pieces
		K	Various Pieces
		GS	Master Series for the Young
	Bagatelle in G, Op. 119, No. 6	I	Bagatelles, Op. 119
		P	Various Pieces
		K	Various Pieces
	Bagatelle in G Minor, Op. 119, No. 1	I	Bagatelles, Op. 119
		P	Various Pieces
		K	Various Pieces
		K	Easy Compositions by Mozart and Beethoven
		GS	Master Series for the Young
	Menuetto, (From Sonata, Op. 2, No. 1)	K	Beethoven Sonatas, Vol. I
		P	
		SS	
		ABR	(Donald Tovey ed.)
		P	Sonaten Album, Vol. II
	Menuetto, (From Sonata, Op. 10, No. 3)		

Composer	Title	Publisher	Volume or Collection
BEETHOVEN, L. van (cont.)	Menuetto, (From Sonata, Op. 31, No. 3)	K P SS ABR	Beethoven Sonatas, Vol. II
	Rondo in A	K P B EHM	Various Pieces Various Pieces Hours with the Masters, Bk. V Discoveries for Piano (Mirovitch)
	Rondo in C, Op. 51, No. 1	K P GS GS GS	Various Pieces Various Pieces Beethoven Easy Compositions Thirty-two Sonatinas and Rondos Introduction to Piano Classics, Vol. II (Mirovitch)
	Scherzo, (From Sonatas, Op. 2, No. 2)	K P SS ABR	Beethoven Sonatas, Vol. I (Donald Tovey ed.)
	Six Ecossaises	P K GS	Beethoven Ecossaisen und Deutsche Tänze Easy Compositions by Mozart and Beethoven Introduction to Piano Classics, Vol. II (Mirovitch)

	Sonata in D
	  Allegro
	  Menuetto
	  Scherzando
		MMC
		He
		K
		MM
		P
			The Three Bonn Sonatas
			The Bonn Sonatas
			Beethoven: Sonatinas
			Published Separately
			Beethoven: Sonatinas

	Sonata in E, Op. 14, No. 1
	  Allegro
	  Allegretto
	  Rondo
		K
		P
		SS
		ABR
		P
			Beethoven Sonatas, Vol. I
			
			(Donald Tovey ed.)
			Sonaten Album, Vol. I

	Sonata in E-flat
	  Allegro cantabile
	  Andante
	  Rondo
		MMC
		He
		K
		P
		MM
			The Three Bonn Sonatas
			The Bonn Sonatas
			Beethoven: Sonatinas
			Beethoven: Sonatinas
			Published Separately

	Sonata in F Minor
	  Larghetto maestoso:
	    Allegro assai
	  Andante
	  Presto
		MMC
		He
		K
		P
		MM
			The Three Bonn Sonatas
			The Bonn Sonatas
			Beethoven: Sonatinas
			Beethoven: Sonatinas
			Published Separately

	Sonata in G Minor, Op. 49, No. 1
	  Andante
	  Rondo
		K
		P
		SS
		ABR
		P
			Beethoven Sonatas, Vol. II
			
			(Donald Tovey ed.)
			Sonaten Album, Vol. I

Composer	Title	Publisher	Volume or Collection
BEETHOVEN, L. van (cont.)		GS CF	Beethoven Easy Compositions Road to Piano Artistry, Vol. IX (Scionti)
	Variations	K P GS	Beethoven Variations, Vol. II
	Eight Variations on "Tandeln und Scherzen"		
	Eight Variations on "Une Fièvre brûlante"		
	Nine Variations on "Quanto è bello"	A	Published Separately
	Six Easy Variations on an Original Theme	A	Published Separately
	Six Variations on "Nel cor più"	A CF P	Published Separately Published Separately Sonatinen Album, Vol. II
	Ten Variations on "La Stessa la stessimissa"		
BORODIN, A. (1834-1887)	Nocturne	P	Petite Suite
	Serenade	P GS	Petite Suite Introduction to Piano Classics, Vol. II (Mirovitch)
BRAHMS, J. (1833-1897)	Hungarian Dance in F, No. 7	GS	Hungarian Dances, Vol. I
	Hungarian Dance in F Sharp Minor, No. 5		
	Two Sarabandes	H	Sarabandes and Gigues
	Waltz in B, Op. 39, No. 1	P I GS	Brahms Waltzes, Op. 39
	Waltz in B Minor, Op. 39, No. 11	P I GS B	Brahms Waltzes, Op. 39 Hours with the Masters, Bk. V
	Waltz in C sharp Minor, Op. 39, No. 7	P I GS	Brahms Waltzes, Op. 39
	Waltz in E, Op. 39, No. 2		
	Waltz in E, Op. 39, No. 10		
	Waltz in E, Op. 39, No. 5	H	Contemporaries of Schumann
CERVANTES, I. (1847-1905)	Six Cuban Dances	GS	Six Cuban Dances

Composer	Title	Publisher	Volume or Collection
CHOPIN, F. (1810-1849)	Marche Funèbre, Op. 72, No. 2	GS	Chopin: Various Compositions
	Mazurkas	GS P K PMP	Mazurkas
	A Minor, Op. 67, No. 4	GS	Master Series for the Young
	A Minor, Op. 68, No. 2	GS	Selected Piano Solos by Romantic Composers, Bk. II
	C Major, Op. 33, No. 3	GS B	Chopin Album for the Piano Hours with the Masters, Bk. IV
	C Major, Op. 68, No. 1	GS	Selected Piano Solos by Romantic Composers, Bk. III
	G Minor, Op. 67, No. 2	GS	Master Series for the Young
	G Minor, Op. 24, No. 1		
	F Major, Op. 63, No. 3	H	Easiest Original Pieces
	F Minor, Op. 63, No. 2	H	Easiest Original Pieces
	Nocturnes	GS P K PMP	Nocturnes
	B-flat Minor, Op. 9, No. 1		
	C-Sharp Minor	GS	Selected Piano Solos by Romantic Composers, Bk. III
	E-Minor, Op. 72, No. 1 (Posth.)		
	E-flat, Op. 9, No. 2	GS	Chopin Album for the Piano
	F Minor, Op. 55, No. 1		
	G Minor, Op. 15, No. 3	GS H	Chopin Album for the Piano Easiest Original Pieces
	G Minor, Op. 37, No. 1	GS	Chopin Album for the Piano
	Polonaise in A, Op. 10, No. 1	GS P K PMP GS GS	Chopin Polonaises Chopin: Twelve Polonaises Chopin Album for the Piano
	Polonaise in C-Minor, Op. 10, No. 2	GS P K PMP	Chopin Polonaises
	Polonaise in C-Sharp Minor, Op. 26, No. 1	GS P K PMP GS	Chopin Polonaises Chopin: Twelve Polonaises
	Prelude in A Minor Op. 28, No. 2	GS K PMP P	Chopin Preludes

Composer	Title	Publisher	Volume or Collection
CHOPIN, F. (cont.)	Prelude in B-flat Op. 28, No. 21		
	Prelude in D-flat, Op. 28, No. 15	GS K P PMP	Chopin Preludes
		GS PP GS H	Chopin Album for the Piano Hundred Best Short Classics, Bk. VI Master Series for the Young Easiest Original Pieces
	Prelude in E, Op. 28, No. 9	GS K PMP P	Chopin Preludes
	Prelude in F Sharp, Op. 28, No. 13	GS K PMP P	Chopin Preludes
	Prelude in G Minor, Op. 28, No. 22	GS K PMP P	Chopin Preludes
	Trois Ecossaises, Op. 72	GS GS	Chopin: Various Compositions Published Separately
	Waltzes	GS P PMP K	Chopin Waltzes
	A Minor, Op. 34, No. 2	GS GS H Sch	Chopin Album for the Piano Selected Piano Solos by Romantic Composers, Bk. III Easiest Original Pieces Published Separately
	A-flat, Op. 69, No. 1		
	B Minor, Op. 69, No. 2		
	C Sharp Minor, Op. 64, No. 2	GS	Chopin Album for the Piano
	D-flat, Op. 64, No. 1	GS Sch	Chopin Album for the Piano Published Separately
	E (Posth.) (Aus dem Nachlasse)	GS	Chopin Album for the Piano
	E Minor (Posth.) (Aus dem Nachlasse)		
	F Minor, Op. 70, No. 2	GS	Master Series for the Young
CLEMENTI, M. (1752-1832)	Andante in B-flat	CF	Road to Piano Artistry, Vol. VIII
	Sonata in A, Op. 36, No. 1 Allegro Presto	GS P	Clementi Sonatas, Bk. I
	Sonata in B-flat, Op. 47, No. 2	GS P	Clementi Sonatas, Bk. II

Composer	Title	Publisher	Volume or Collection
CLEMENTI, M. (cont.)	Allegro con brio Andante quasi allegretto Rondo		
	Sonata in D, Op. 26, No. 3 Presto Un poco andante Rondo	GS P	Clementi Sonatas, Bk. I
	Sonatina in G, Op. 36, No. 5 Presto Air Suisse Rondo	GS P GS GS P	Clementi: Six Sonatinas, Op. 36 Album of Sonatinas Thirty-two Sonatinas and Rondos Sonatinas, Vol. I
	Sonatina in D, Op. 36, No. 6 Allegro con spirito Rondo	GS P K GS CF GS P	Clementi: Six Sonatinas, Op. 36 Selected Sonatinas, Bk. II Road to Piano Artistry, Vol. VI (Scionti) Thirty-two Sonatinas and Rondos Sonatinen Album, Vol. I
FIELD, J. (1782-1837)	Nocturne in C, No. 17	GS P	Field: Eighteen Nocturnes Field Nocturnes
	Nocturne in C Minor, No. 2	GS P	Field: Eighteen Nocturnes Field Nocturnes
	Nocturne in D Minor, No. 15	GS P GS	Field: Eighteen Nocturnes Field Nocturnes Selected Piano Solos by Romantic Composers, Bk. I
	Nocturne in E Minor, No. 9	GS P GS	Field: Eighteen Nocturnes Field Nocturnes Selected Piano Solos by Romantic Composers, Bk. III
	Nocturne in E-flat, No. 1	GS P R	Field: Eighteen Nocturnes Field Nocturnes Published Separately
	Nocturne in F, No. 18	GS P GS	Field: Eighteen Nocturnes Field Nocturnes Selected Piano Solos by Romantic Composers, Bk. II
GALLÉS, J. (1781-1836)	Sonata in C Minor	Su	Portuguese and Spanish Keyboard Music
GRIEG, E. (1843-1907)	Albumleaf, Op. 28, No. 1	GS P GS	Album-Leaves, Op. 28 Forty-five Selected Compositions for Piano, Bk. II
	Albumleaf, Op. 28, No. 4	GS P GS	Album-Leaves, Op. 28 Forty-five Selected Compositions for Piano, Bk. II

Composer	Title	Publisher	Volume or Collection
GRIEG, E. (cont.)	Albumleaf, Op. 47, No. 2	P GS GS	Lyrical Pieces, Op. 47 Forty-five Selected Compositions for Piano, Bk. I
	Carnival Scene, Op. 19, No. 3	P GS	Sketches of Norwegian Life, Op. 19

	Holberg Suite, Op. 40
	  1. Prelude
	  2. Sarabande
	  3. Gavotte
	  4. Air
	  5. Rigaudon
		P
		GS
			Holberg Suite, Op. 40
			From Holberg's Time, Op. 40

	March of the Dwarfs, Op. 54, No. 3	P GS K	Lyrical Pieces, Op. 54
	Mélancolie, Op. 47, No. 5	P GS GS	Lyrical Pieces, Op. 47 Forty-five Selected Compositions for Piano, Bk. I
	Norwegian Dance, Op. 54, No. 2	P GS K	Lyrical Pieces, Op. 54
	On the Mountains, Op. 19, No. 1	P GS	Sketches of Norwegian Life
	Scherzo, Op. 54, No. 5	P GS K GS	Lyrical Pieces, Op. 54 Forty-five Selected Compositions, Bk. 2
	Shepherd's Boy, Op. 54, No. 1	P GS K	Lyrical Pieces, Op. 54
	Spring Dance, Op. 47, No. 6	P GS GS	Lyrical Pieces, Op. 47 Forty-five Selected Compositions for Piano, Bk. II
	To Spring, Op. 43, No. 6	P GS K GS CF	Lyrical Pieces, Op. 43 Forty-five Selected Compositions for Piano, Bk. II Road to Piano Artistry, Vol. VIII (Scionti)
	Traveller's Song, Op. 17, No. 13	P GS	Northern Dances and Folk Tunes, Op. 17 Master Series for the Young
	Valse Impromptu, Op. 47, No. 1	P GS	Lyrical Pieces, Op. 47
HELLER, S. (1813-1888)	A Narrative, Op. 46, No. 30	R GS	Thirty Progressive Studies, Op. 46
	Gipsies III	CF	Road to Piano Artistry, Vol. V (Scionti)

Composer	Title	Publisher	Volume or Collection
HUMMEL, J. N. (1778-1837)	Rondo in E-flat, Op. 11	GS	Published Separately
KUHLAU, F. (1786-1832)	Rondo in F, Op. 40, No. 3	GS	Thirty-two Sonatinas and Rondos
	Sonatina in A, Op. 59, No. 1 Allegro Rondo	GS	Kuhlau Sonatinas, Bk. I
	Sonatina in A, Op. 60, No. 2 Allegro con spirito Allegro moderato	GS	Kuhlau Sonatinas, Bk. II
	Sonatina in C, Op. 59, No. 3 Allegro con spirito Rondo	GS	Kuhlau Sonatinas, Bk. I
	Sonatina in C, Op. 60, No. 3 Allegro Allegro vivace	GS	Kuhlau Sonatinas, Bk. II
	Sonatina in F, Op. 59, No. 2 Allegro Rondo	GS	Kuhlau Sonatinas, Bk. I
	Sonatina in F, Op. 60, No. 1 Allegro Allegro	GS	Kuhlau Sonatinas, Bk. II
LISZT, F. (1811-1886)	Au Lac de Wallenstadt	GS GS	Annés de Pèlerinage, Bk. I: Premiere Année "Suisse" Selected Piano Solos by Romantic Composers, Bk. III
	Christmas Tree 1. An Old Christmas Carol 2. The Shepherds at the Manger 3. Chimes 4. In Olden Times 5. Old Provencal Christmas Carol	MP	Liszt: Christmas Tree
	Consolation in E, No. 5	GS PP CF	Consolations; Liebesträume Hundred Best Short Classics, Bk. IV Road to Piano Artistry, Vol. VII (Scionti)
	Consolations. Nos. 2, 3, 4, 5, 6	GS	Consolations; Liebesträume
	Liebesträume in A-flat, No. 3	GS GS	Consolations; Liebesträume Published Separately
	Liebesträume in E, No. 2	GS	Consolations; Liebesträume
MACDOWELL, E. (1861-1908)	By A Meadow Brook, Op. 51, No. 9	Sch GS M I K	Woodland Sketches, Op. 51

Composer	Title	Publisher	Volume or Collection

MACDOWELL. E. (cont.)	Four Little Poems, Op. 32
	  1. The Eagle
	  2. The Brook
	  3. Moonshine
	  4. Winter
		AMP
		GS
		CF
			Four Little Poems

	From "Twelve Etudes"
	  4. Arabesque
	  5. In the Forest
	  6. Dance of the
	     Gnomes
	  7. Idyll
	  8. Shadow Dance
	  9. Intermezzo
	  10. Melody
	  11. Scherzino
	  12. Hungarian
		BMC
		
		I
		Su
			Twelve Etudes, Op. 59
			
			Published Separately

	In Autumn, Op. 51, No. 4	Sch GS M I K	Woodland Sketches, Op. 51
	March Wind, Op. 46, No. 10	AMP AMP	Twelve Virtuoso Studies, Op. 46 Published Separately
	Polonaise, Op. 46, No. 12	AMP AMP	Twelve Virtuoso Studies, Op. 46 Published Separately
	The Joy of Autumn Op. 62, No. 10	K GS	New England Idylls, Op. 62
	Will O' The Wisp. Op. 51, No. 2	Sch GS M I K	Woodland Sketches, Op. 51
	Witches Dance, Op. 17, No. 2	GS K	Published Separately
MENDELSSOHN, F. (1809-1847)	Albumleaf, Op. 117	P	Mendelssohn, Vol. 5, Supplement
	Andante, Op. 16, No. 3	CF	Road to Piano Artistry, Vol. IX (Scionti)
	Andante cantabile	GS GS	Mendelssohn: Miscellaneous Compositions (Kullak) Master Series for the Young
	Characteristic Piece, Op. 7, No. 6 (With Longing)	GS GS	Mendelssohn: Miscellaneous Compositions (Kullak) Master Series for the Young
	Etude, Op. 104, No. 1	GS CF	Three Etudes from Op. 104 Road to Piano Artistry, Vol. IX (Scionti)
	Fantasy or Caprice, Op. 16, No. 1	GS	Mendelssohn: Miscellaneous Compositions (Kullak)

Composer	Title	Publisher	Volume or Collection
MENDELSSOHN, F. (cont.)		A	Beringer's School of Easy Classics: Mendelssohn
	Retrospection, Op. 102, No. 2	P GS Wo	Songs Without Words
		GS	Introduction to Piano Classics, Vol. III (Mirovitch)
	Reverie, Op. 85, No. 1	P GS Wo	Songs Without Words
		GS	Selected Piano Solos by Romantic Composers, Bk. III
	Rondo Capriccioso, Op. 14	GS	Mendelssohn: Miscellaneous Compositions (Kullak)
		GS	Published Separately
	Scherzo, Op. 16, No. 2	GS	Mendelssohn: Miscellaneous Compositions (Kullak)
		GS	Published Separately
	Songs Without Words	P GS Wo	Songs Without Words

Op. 19
1. Sweet Remembrance
3. Hunting Song
5. Restlessness

Op. 30
1. Contemplation
2. Unrest
4. The Wanderer
5. The Brook

Op. 38
1. Evening Star
2. Lost Happiness
3. The Poet's Harp
5. Passion
6. Duet

Op. 53
1. On The Seashore
2. Fleecy Clouds
3. Agitation
5. Folk Song
6. The Flight

Op. 62
1. May Breezes
2. The Departure
3. Funeral March
5. Venetian Boat Song III

Op. 67
1. Meditation
2. Lost Illusions

Composer	Title	Publisher	Volume or Collection
MENDELSSOHN, F. (cont.)	3. Song of the Pilgrim 4. Spinning Song 6. Lullaby		

	Op. 85
	  1. Reverie
	  2. The Adieu
	  3. Delirium
	  4. Elegy
	  5. The Return
	  6. Song of the Traveller		

	Op. 102
	  1. Homeless
	  2. Retrospection
	  4. The Sighing Wind
	  5. The Joyous Peasant		

	Sweet Remembrance, Op. 19, No. 1	GS	Introduction to Piano Classics, Bk. III (Mirovitch)
	Two Musical Sketches	A	Beringer's School of Easy Classics: Mendelssohn
	Venetian Boat Song III, Op. 62, No. 5	P Wo GS GS	Songs Without Words Selected Piano Solos by Romantic Composers, Bk. III
SCHUBERT, F. (1797-1828)	Allegretto in C Minor	GS H Ho	Master Series for the Young Easiest Original Pieces Published Separately
	Andante (From Sonata Op. 120)	K P GS P GS H	Sonatas, Vol. I Sonatinen Album, Vol. II Master Series for the Young Easiest Original Pieces
	Impromptu in A-flat, Op. 90, No. 4	GS P P PP Sch GS	Four Impromptus, Op. 90 Impromptus, Op. 90 Impromptus and Moments Musicaux Hundred Best Short Classics, Bk. IV Published Separately Published Separately
	Impromptu in A-flat, Op. 142, No. 2	P GS P P	Impromptus, Op. 142 Impromptus, Op. 90 and Op. 142 Impromptus and Moments Musicaux
	Impromptu in E-flat, Op. 90, No. 2	GS P P P Sch GS	Four Impromptus, Op. 90 Impromptus, Op. 90 Impromptus, Op. 90 and Op. 142 Impromptus and Moments Musicaux Published Separately Published Separately

Composer	Title	Publisher	Volume or Collection
SCHUBERT, F. (cont.)	Menuet (From Sonata Op. 122)	K	Sonatas, Vol. I
		P	
		GS	
		A	Beringer's School of Easy Classics: Schubert
	Moment Musicial in A-flat, Op. 94, No. 6	P	Moments Musicaux, Op. 94
		GS	
		P	Impromptus and Moments Musicaux
		GS	Published Separately
		GS	Selected Piano Solos by Romantic Composers, Bk. III
	Moment Musical in F Minor, Op. 94, No. 3	P	Moments Musicaux, Op. 94
		GS	
		P	Impromptus and Moments Musicaux
		JF	Published Separately
		GS	Published Separately
		GS	Master Series for the Young
		PP	Hundred Best Short Classics, Bk. IV
	Scherzo in A, (From Five Piano Pieces)	K	Schubert: Various Pieces
	Scherzo in D-flat	GS	Introduction to Piano Classics, Vol. III (Mirovitch)
	Waltzes, Op. 77 (Complete) (12 Valses Nobles)	P	Schubert Dances
		GS	
	Waltzes, Op. 127 (Complete) (13 last waltzes)	P	Schubert Dances
		GS	
	5. F Major	A	Beringer's School of Easy Classics: Schubert
	Waltz in B, Op. 18a, No. 2	P	Schubert Dances
		GS	
		GS	Introduction to Piano Classics, Vol. III (Mirovitch)
	Waltz in E, Op. 18a, No. 1	P	Schubert Dances
		GS	
		GS	Introduction to Piano Classics, Vol. III (Mirovitch)
	Waltz in E, Op. 18a, No. 11	P	Schubert Dances
		GS	
		GS	Introduction to Piano Classics, Vol. III (Mirovitch)
	Waltz in F sharp minor, Op. 18a, No. 8	P	Schubert Dances
		GS	
		GS	Introduction to Piano Classics, Vol. III (Mirovitch)
	Waltz in G, Op. 18a, No. 3	P	Schubert Dances
		GS	
		GS	Introduction to Piano Classics, Vol. III

Composer	Title	Publisher	Volume or Collection
SCHUBERT, F. (cont.)	Waltzes (selected) Sets III and V	JF	Schubert Waltzes (Maier)
	Variations on a Theme by Anselm Huttenbrenner	K	Schubert: Various Pieces
SCHUMANN, R. (1810-1856)	A Message, Op. 124, No. 18	K GS	Complete Works, Vol. VI Album Leaves, Op. 124
	Album Leaves, Op. 99 1. Ziemlich langsam 2. Schnell 3. Ziemlich langsam 4. Sehr langsam 5. Langsam	GS K	Colored Leaves, Op. 99 Complete Works, Vol. VI
	Almost Too Serious, Op. 15, No. 10	GS P AMP K	Scenes from Childhood, Op. 15 Complete Works, Vol. III
	Arabesque, Op. 18	K AMP GS P	Complete Works, Vol. III Published Separately
	At The Fireside, Op. 15, No. 8	GS P AMP K	Scenes from Childhood, Op. 15 Complete Works, Vol. III
	Burla, Op. 124, No. 12	K GS	Complete Works, Vol. VI Album Leaves, Op. 124
	Canon, Op. 124, No. 20	GS K	Album Leaves, Op. 124 Complete Works, Vol. VI
	Catch Me, Op. 15, No. 3	GS P AMP B	Scenes From Childhood, Op. 15 Hours with the Masters, Bk. V
	Child Falling Asleep, Op. 15, No. 12	GS P AMP CF	Scenes From Childhood, Op. 15 Road to Piano Artistry, Vol. IX (Scionti)
	Country Dance, Op. 124, No. 7	GS K H	Album Leaves, Op. 124 Complete Works, Vol. VI Easiest Original Pieces
	Entreating Child, Op. 15, No. 4	GS P AMP PP	Scenes From Childhood, Op. 15 Hundred Best Short Classics, Bk. V
	Evening Music, Op. 99, No. 6	GS K	Colored Leaves, Op. 99 Complete Works, Vol. VI
	Fantastic Dance, Op. 124, No. 5	GS K	Album Leaves, Op. 124 Complete Works Vol. VI

Composer	Title	Publisher	Volume or Collection
SCHUMANN, R. (cont.)		H	Easiest Original Pieces
		JF	Published Separately
	Fantastic Piece, Op. 124, No. 19	GS	Album Leaves, Op. 124
		K	Complete Works, Vol. VI
		B	Hours with the Masters, Bk. 5
	Figured Choral, Op. 68, No. 42	P	Album for the Young, Op. 68
		GS	
	Forebodings, Op. 124, No. 2	GS	Album Leaves, Op. 124
		K	Complete Works, Vol. VI
	Frightening, Op. 15, No. 11	GS	Scenes From Childhood, Op. 15
		AMP	
		P	
	Grief's Forebodings, Op. 124, No. 8	GS	Album Leaves, Op. 124
		H	Easiest Original Pieces
		K	Complete Works, Vol. VI
	Grillen, Op. 12, No. 4	GS	Fantasy Pieces, Op. 12
		P	
		AMP	
		K	Complete Works, Vol. II
	Hunting Song, Op. 82, No. 7	GS	Forest Scenes, Op. 82
		AMP	
		K	Complete Works, Vol. V
		GS	Published Separately
	Impromptu, Op. 124, No. 1	GS	Album Leaves, Op. 124
		K	Complete Works, Vol. VI
	Knight of the Hobbyhorse, Op. 15, No. 9	GS	Scenes From Childhood, Op. 15
		AMP	
		P	
	Larghetto, Op. 124, No. 13	GS	Album Leaves, Op. 124
		K	Complete Works, Vol. VI
	Nachtstücke, Op. 23, No. 4	GS	Four Nachtstücke
		K	Complete Works, Vol. IV
		PP	Hundred Best Short Classics, Bk. VI
		GS	Published Separately
	Novellette, Op. 21	GS	Eight Novelleten, Op. 21
		P	
		AMP	
		K	Complete Works, Vol. IV
		GS	Published Separately
	Novelette, Op. 99	GS	Colored Leaves, Op. 99
		K	Complete Works, Vol. VI
		GS	Published Separately (No. 3)
	Perfectly Contented, Op. 15, No. 5	GS	Scenes From Childhood, Op. 15
		AMP	
		P	
		PP	Hundred Best Short Classics, Bk. V

Composer	Title	Publisher	Volume or Collection
SCHUMANN, R. (cont.)	Romance in F sharp, Op. 28, No. 2	GS AMP PP	Three Romances Hundred Best Short Classics, Bk. VI
	Romance, Op. 124, No. 11	GS K	Album Leaves, Op. 124 Complete Works, Vol. VI
	Scherzino, Op. 124, No. 3	GS K	Album Leaves, Op. 124 Complete Works, Vol. VI
	Scherzo, Gigue, Romance, and Fughetta, Op. 32	GS K	Scherzo, Gigue, Romance and Fughetta, Op. 32 Complete Works, Vol. IV
	Slumber Song, Op. 124, No. 16	GS K A GS	Album Leaves, Op. 124 Complete Works, Vol. VI Beringer's School of Easy Classics: Schumann Published Separately
	Soaring, Op. 12, No. 2	GS AMP P K	Fantasy Pieces, Op. 12 Complete Works, Vol. II
	Sonata II, Op. 118b Allegro Canon Evening Song Children's Party	GS K	Three Sonatas for the Young, Op. 118 Complete Works, Vol. VI
	Sonata III, Op. 118c Allegro Andante Gipsy Dance A Child's Dream	GS K	Three Sonatas for the Young, Op. 118 Complete Works, Vol. VI
	The Elf, Op. 124, No. 17	GS K A	Album Leaves, Op. 124 Complete Works, Vol. VI Beringer's School of Easy Classics: Schumann
	The Poet Speaks, Op. 15, No. 13	GS P AMP	Scenes From Childhood, Op. 15
	The Prophet Bird, Op. 82 No. 6	AMP GS K PP GS	Forest Scenes, Op. 82 Complete Works, Vol. V Hundred Best Short Classics, Bk. VII Selected Piano Solos by Romantic Composers, Bk. III
	Three Little Pieces, Op. 99 1. Nicht schnell 3. Frisch	GS K	Colored Leaves, Op. 99 Complete Works, Vol. VI
	Traumerei, Op. 15, No. 7	GS AMP P K	Scenes From Childhood, Op. 15 Complete Works, Vol. III

Composer	Title	Publisher	Volume or Collection
SCHUMANN, R. (cont.)		PP	Hundred Best Short Classics, Bk. IV
		GS	Published Separately
	Variations on an Original Theme	H	Variations on an Original Theme
	Vision, Op. 124, No. 14	GS	Album Leaves, Op. 124
		K	Complete Works, Vol. VI
	Waltz, Op. 99, No. 3	GS	Colored Leaves, Op. 99
		K	Complete Works, Vol. VI
	Waltz, Op. 124, No. 10	GS	Album Leaves, Op. 124
		K	Complete Works, Vol. VI
	Waltz, Op. 124, No. 15	GS	Album Leaves, Op. 124
		K	Complete Works, Vol. VI
	Warum, Op. 12, No. 3	GS	Fantasy Pieces, Op. 12
		AMP	
		P	
		K	Complete Works, Vol. II
		PP	Hundred Best Short Classics, Bk. VII
TSCHAIKOWSKY, P. (1840-1893)	August - Harvest Song, Op. 37a, No. 8	GS	The Seasons, Op. 37a
		P	
	December - Christmas, Op. 37a, No. 12	GS	The Seasons, Op. 37a
		P	
		GS	Selected Piano Solos by Romantic Composers, Bk. II
	February - Carnival, Op. 37a, No. 2	GS	The Seasons, Op. 37a
		P	
	July - Song of the Reaper, Op. 37a, No. 7	GS	The Seasons, Op. 37a
		P	
	June - Barcarolle, Op. 37a, No. 6	GS	The Seasons, Op. 37a
		P	
		GS	Selected Piano Solos by Romantic Composers, Bk. III
		GS	Published Separately
	March - Song of the Lark, Op. 37a, No. 3	GS	The Seasons, Op. 37a
		P	
	Nocturne in C Sharp Minor, Op. 19, No. 4	GS	Introduction to Piano Classics, Vol. II (Mirovitch)
		GS	Published Separately
	November - Troika, Op. 37a, No. 11	GS	The Seasons, Op. 37a
		P	
		GS	Introduction to Piano Classics, Vol. II (Mirovitch)
	September - Hunter's Song, Op. 37a, No. 9	GS	The Seasons, Op. 37a
		P	
WEBER, C. (1786-1826)	Mazurka, Op. 10, No. 4	GS	Master Series for the Young
	Rondo, Op. 3, No. 6	GS	Master Series for the Young

Composer	Title	Publisher	Volume or Collection

AURIC, GEORGES (1899-)	Petite Suite
	  1. Prelude
	  2. Danse
	  3. Vilanelle et Entrée
	  4. Sarabande
	  5. Voltes
		HC	Petite Suite

BARTÓK. BÉLA (1881-1945)	An Air	BH	Nine Little Piano Pieces, Bk. II
	Bagatelles, Op. 6, Nos. 2, 5, 8, 9, 11, 13, 14	BH GS	Fourteen Bagatelles, Op. 6 Bartók--Selected Works for the Piano
	From "Four Dirges," Op. 8b Nos. 2, 3 and 4	BH GS	Four Dirges, Op. 8b Bartók--Selected Works for the Piano
	Mikrokosmos, Vol. V A Bagpipe	BH	Mikrokosmos. Vol. V
	Mikrokosmos, Vol. VI Ostinato	BH	Mikrokosmos, Vol. VI
	Roumanian Folk Dances Nos. 5 and 6	BH GS	Roumanian Folk Dances Bartók--Selected Works for the Piano

	Sonatina
	  Bagpipers
	  Bear Dance
	  Finale
		BH
		Su
		
		I
			Sonatina
			Contemporary Piano Literature, Bk. 6
			  (Clark)

	Three Rondos	BH	Three Rondos on Folk Tunes
	Tambourine	BH	Nine Little Piano Pieces, Bk. II

BATE, STANLEY (1912-)	Six Pieces for an Infant Prodigy
	  1. Very Fast
	  2. Very Simply
	  3. In Quick March Time
	  4. Moderately
	  5. Quickly
	  6. Very Fast
		MP	Six Pieces for an Infant Prodigy

	Seven Pieces for Piano
	  1. Prelude
	  2. Romance
	  3. Chanson Populaire
	  4. Moment Musicale
	  5. Polka
	  6. Melodie
	  7. Valse
		Sch	Seven Pieces for Piano

	Sonatina No. 7 1. March	Sch	Sonatina, No. 7

Composer	Title	Publisher	Volume or Collection
BATE, STANLEY (cont.)	2. Pastoral 3. Tarantella		

CARPENTER, JOHN ALDEN (1876-1951)	From "Diversions"
	  1. Lento
	  2. Allegretto con moto
	  4. Moderato
		GS	Diversions

CASTILLO, RICARDO (1894-)	Canción del Pescador Scherzo (Evolucion del sol)	EV	6 Modern Guatemalan Composers

CASTRO, JOSÉ MARIA (1909-)	From "Diez Breves"
	  1. Estudio
	  2. Canción de Cuna
	  3. Circo
	  4. Campanas
		GS	Latin American Art Music

COPLAND, AARON (1900-)	The Cat and the Mouse (Scherzo Humoristique)	BH	Published Separately

COWELL, HENRY (1897-)	Celtic Set
	  1. Rul
	  2. Caoine
	  3. Hornpipe
		CF	Celtic Set

DEBUSSY, CLAUDE (1862-1918)	Arabesques
	
	  1. E Major
	
	  2. G Major
		EV
		I
		I
		GS
		I
		GS
			Deux Arabesques
			2 Arabesques
			Published Separately
			Published Separately
			Published Separately
			Published Separately

	Clair de Lune	EV EV I GS	Suite bergamasque Published Separately Published Separately Published Separately
	Danseuses de Delphes	EV EV	Preludes, Bk. I Published Separately
	Golliwog's Cakewalk	EV M EV	Children's Corner Published Separately
	Jimbo's Lullaby	EV M EV	Children's Corner Published Separately
	La Cathédrale engloutie	EV EV	Preludes, Bk. I Published Separately
	La Fille aux cheveux de lin	EV EV	Preludes, Bk. I Published Separately
	La Plus que lente	EV	Published Separately
	Little Nigar	EV M	Published Separately

Composer	Title	Publisher	Volume or Collection
DEBUSSY, CLAUDE (cont.)	Little Shepherd	EV M	Published Separately
	Rêverie	EV M	Published Separately
		GS	51 Piano Pieces from the Modern Repertoire
	Serenade for the Doll	EV EV	Children's Corner Published Separately
	Valse romantique	EV GS	Published Separately 51 Piano Pieces from the Modern Repertoire
DELLO JOIO, NORMAN (1913-)	Prelude: To a Young Dancer	GS	Published Separately
	Prelude: To a Young Musician	GS	Published Separately
DETT, R. NATHANIEL (1882-1943)	Juba Dance	Su	Published Separately
DIAMOND, DAVID (1915-)	Sonatina 1. Largo assai 2. Allegretto 3. Allegro vivace	MP	Sonatina
DOHNANYI, ERNST VON (1877-1960)	From "Bagatelles," Op. 13 1. Dedication 2. March 3. To Ada 7. At Midnight 9. Dawn 10. Postlude	Do M	Winterreigen, Ten Bagatelles, Op. 13 Published Separately
FABINI, F. E. (1883-)	Trieste, No. 2	GS	Latin American Art Music
FICHER, JACABO (1896-)	From "Six Animal Fables," Op. 38 1. The Arrogant Rooster and the Humble Hen 2. Lullaby for a Cat 3. Pussy-Cat and Nanny-Goat	Ax	Published Separately
FULEIHAN, ANIS (1900-)	Short Pieces 1. Madrigal 4. Rhythmic Episode 5. Slow Waltz 6. Five-Eight 7. Invention 8. Scherzino 10. Conversation	CF	Fifteen Short Pieces

Composer	Title	Publisher	Volume or Collection
FULEIHAN, ANIS (cont.)	12. Plaintive Waltz 14. Reflection		

GIANNEO, LUIS (1897-)	From "Petites Pièces"
	  1. Coquettirei
	  5. Mouvement Per-
	      pétual
		E	Cinq Petites Pièces

GINASTERA, ALBERTO (1916-)	Creole Dance	CF	12 American Preludes, Vol. I
	Pequeña Danza	BA	Published Separately

	Piezas Infantiles
	  1. Antón Pirulero
	  2. Chacarerita
	  3. Arroz con Leche
		GS	Latin American Art Music

	Rondo on Argentine Children's Folk Tunes	BH	Published Separately

	Two Pieces from "Danzas
	Argentinas"
	  1. Danza del viejo
	      boyero
	  2. Danza de la moza
	      donosa
		D	Danzas Argentinas

	Two Preludes
	  9. Tribute to Aaron
	      Copland
	  10. Postlude
		CF	Twelve American Preludes, Vol. II

GODOWSKY, LEOPOLD (1870-1938)	Nocturnal Tangier	GS GS	51 Piano Pieces from the Modern Reper- toire Published Separately

GOOSSENS, EUGENE (1893-1962)	From "Kaleidoscope,"
	Op. 18
	  1. Good Morning
	  2. Promenade
	  4. March of the Wooden
	      Soldier
	  5. The Rocking Horse
	  6. The Punch and Judy
	      Show
	  7. A Ghost Story
	  12. Good Night
		C
		M
			Kaleidoscope, Op. 18

GRANADOS, ENRIQUE (1867-1916)	Spanish Dances
	  1. Minueto
	  2. Oriental
	  3. Zarabanda
	  4. Villanesca
	  5. Andaluza (Playera)
	  6. Jota (Rondalla
	      Aragonese)
	  7. Valenciana
		MMC
		
		UME
		
		UME
		UME
		UME
			Twelve Spanish Dances, Op. 5
			
			Published Separately
			
			Published Separately
			Published Separately
			Published Separately

Composer	Title	Publisher	Volume or Collection
GRANADOS, ENRIQUE (cont.)	8. Asturiana 9. Mazurca 10. Danza Triste 11. Zambra 12. Arabesca (Mélancolica)		
GREEN, RAY (1909-)	Short Sonata in F 1. Opening Movement 2. Pastorale 3. Chorale 4. Ending Movement	AME	Short Sonata in F
GRIFFES, CHARLES (1884-1920)	The Lake at Evening	GS	Published Separately
GROVLEZ, GABRIEL (1879-1944)	From "A Child's Garden" 1. La Sieste 2. Choses du Soir 3. Chanson de Grand- Père 6. Pepita	C	A Child's Garden

	L'Aimanach Aux Images
	1. Les Marionettes
	2. Berceuse de la
	   Poupée
	3. La Sarabande
	4. Chanson du Chas-
	   seur
	5. Les Anes
	6. Le Pastour
	7. Chanson de
	   l'Escarpolette
	8. Petites Letaines De
	   Jésus
		A	L'Almanach Aux Images

GUARNIERE, C. (1907-)	Ficarás Sosinha	MMC	Published Separately
GUION, DAVID (1895-)	The Harmonica Player (From "Alley Tunes")	GS	Published Separately
HANSON, HOWARD (1896-)	Clog Dance	CF	Published Separately
HERRATE, MANUEL (1924-)	From "Six Sketches" Nos. 1, 2 and 5	EV	Six Sketches for Piano
	Tres Danzas Para Piano 1. Allegro 2. Andantino 3. Presto	PAU	Tres Danzas Para Piano
HOLTZMANN, R. (1910-)	Pequeña Suite 1. Preludio Pastoral	ECI	Pequeña Suite

Composer	Title	Publisher	Volume or Collection
HOLTZMANN, R. (cont.)	2. Bailan Las Mu-chachas 3. Melodia Triste 4. Fanfarria Campestre 5. Interludio Evocativo		
IBERT, J. (1895-1962)	From "Histoires" 2. Le petit âne blanc (The Little White Donkey) 4. A Giddy Girl 5. Dans la maison triste 7. Bajo la mesa 8. La cage de cristal 9. La Marchande d'eau fraîche 10. Le Cortège de Balkis	Le	Histoires Published Separately Published Separately
IRELAND, JOHN (1879-1962)	The Island Spell	A	Published Separately
ITURBI, JOSE (1895-)	Pequeña Danza Española	GS	Published Separately
KABALEVSKY, DMITRI (1904-)	Preludes 1. C Major 2. A Minor 3. E Minor 8. A Major 9. E Major 15. D-flat Major 20. C Minor 23. F Major	I	24 Preludes, Op. 38
	Sonatina in C, Op. 13, No. 1 1. Allegro assai e lusingando 2. Andantino 3. Presto	L I GS P Su	Published Separately Contemporary Piano Literature, Bk. 6 (Clark)
KENNAN, KENT (1913-)	Three Preludes	GS	Three Preludes for the Piano
KRENEK, ERNEST (1900-)	Little Suite, Op. 13a 1. Allemande 2. Sarabande 3. Gavotte 4. Waltz 5. Fugue 6. Fox Trot	K	Little Suite, Op. 13a

Composer	Title	Publisher	Volume or Collection
MEDTNER, NIKOLAI (1879-1959)	Fairy Tale, Op. 14, No. 1	MMC M I	Published Separately Album of Selected Pieces: Medtner

MILHAUD, DARIUS (1892-)	Saudades do Brazil, Vol. I
	  1. Sorocabo
	  2. Botafogo
	  3. Leme
	  4. Copacabana
	  5. Ipanema
	  6. Gavea
	
	  Vol. II
	  7. Corcovada
	  8. Tijuca
	  9. Sumaré
	 10. Paineras
	 11. Larendeiras
	 12. Paysandú
		E	Saudades do Brazil

MOMPOU, FEDERICO (1893-)	Cancó I Dansa (Song and Dance) Part I	M UME	Published Separately

	Scènes d'Enfants
	  1. Cris dans la rue
	  2. Jeux sur la plage
	  3. Jeu
	  4. Jeu
	  5. Jeunes filles au jardin
		S	Scènes d'Enfants

MOORE, DOUGLAS (1893-)	Museum Piece	Co	Published Separately

	Suite
	  Dancing School
	  Prelude
	  Processional
	  Reel
		CF	Published Separately

MORILLO, ROBERTO (1911-)	Canción Triste y Danza Alegri	GS	Latin American Art Music
PALMGREN, SELIM (1878-1951)	Cradle Song	BMC	Published Separately

	Five Sketches, Op. 31
	  1. Karelian Dance
	  2. Minuet
	  3. A Guilty Conscience
	  4. Minuet Waltz
	  5. Finlandish Dance
		BMC	Sketches from Finland, Op. 31

	May Night	BMC	Published Separately

	Six Lyric Pieces, Op. 28
	  1. Preludium
	  2. The Isle of Shadows
	  3. Legend
		BMC	Six Lyric Pieces, Op. 28

Composer	Title	Publisher	Volume or Collection
PALMGREN, SELIM (cont.)	4. A Mother's Song 5. The Swan 6. Roundelay		
PERSICHETTI, VINCENT (1915-)	Variations for an Album	MP	Published Separately
PINTO, OCTAVIO (1890-1950)	From "Memories of Child-hood" 1. Run, Run 2. Ring Around the Rosy 5. Hobby Horse	GS	Memories of Childhood
	Tom Thumb's March	GS GS	Published Separately 51 Pieces from the Modern Repertoire
POULENC, FRANCIS (1889-1963)	Mouvements perpétuels	C	Mouvements perpétuels
PROKOFIEFF, SERGE (1891-1953)	Gavotte, Op. 12, No. 2	GS	Published Separately
	March, Op. 12, No. 1	GS	Published Separately
	Prelude, Op. 12, No. 7	GS	Published Separately
	Tales of the Old Grand-mother, Op. 31 1. Moderato 2. Andantino 3. Andante assai 4. Sostenuto	L AMP K BH	Tales of the Old Grandmother, Op. 31
REBIKOV, VLADIMIR (1866-1920)	Les Démons s'amusent	GS MMC	51 Piano Pieces from the Modern Repertoire Published Separately
RESPIGHI, OTTORINO (1879-1936)	Notturno	GS GS	Published Separately 51 Piano Pieces from the Modern Repertoire
REUTTER, HERMANN (1900-)	Variations on a Children's Song, Op. 28	Sch	The New Piano Book. Vol. II
ROZSA, MIKLOS (1907-)	From "Kaleidoscope," Op. 19 Burlesque Zingara	AMP	Published Separately
SATIE, ERIK (1866-1925)	Sonatine Bureaucratique Allegro Andante Vivace	EV	Sonatine Bureaucratique

Composer	Title	Publisher	Volume or Collection
SCHMITT, FLORENT (1870-1958)	Pacing	CF	Published Separately
SCHOENBERG, A. (1874-1951)	Six Little Piano Pieces, Op. 19	AMP	Six Little Piano Pieces, Op. 19: Schoenberg
SCOTT, CYRIL (1879-)	Danse Négre, Op. 58, No. 5	G	Published Separately
	Dance of the Elephants	Sch	Impressions from the Jungle Book
	Guttersnipes' Dance	Sch	The New Piano Book, Vol. III
	Lento from "Two Pierrot Pieces"	BH	Published Separately
	Lotus Land, Op. 47, No. 1	G	Published Separately
	Rikki-Tikki-Tavi and the Snake	Sch	Impressions from the Jungle Book
SCRIABINE, ALEXANDER (1872-1915)	Preludes, Op. 11	MMC M I BH	Preludes, Op. 11
	2. A Minor 4. E Minor 9. E Major 10. C Sharp Minor 13. G-flat Major 15. D-flat Major 17. A-flat Major 22. G Minor		
SÉVÉRAC, D. de (1873-1921)	From "En Vacances" Series I	S	En Vacances—Series I
	6. An Old Music Box	S	Published Separately
	7. Romantic Waltz	S	Published Separately
SHOSTAKOVITCH, DMITRI (1906-)	Polka, Op. 22	L GS I	Published Separately 51 Piano Pieces from the Modern Repertoire Album of Selected Piano Works (Shostakovitch)
	Preludes, Op. 34, Nos. 2, 7, 13, 14, 15, 16, 17, 19, 22, 24	L I W	Twenty-four Preludes, Op. 34
	Three Fantastic Dances, Op. 1	L GS M I	Three Fantastic Dances, Op. I Album of Selected Piano Works: Shostakovitch
SIBELIUS, JAN (1865-1957)	Air Castles (Prelude) Op. 46, No. 1	BMC	From The Land of a Thousand Lakes

Composer	Title	Publisher	Volume or Collection
SIBELIUS, JEAN (cont.)	Alla Gavotta, Op. 46, No. 7		
	Love Sorrow, Op. 57, No. 2		
	Nocturne, Op. 51, No. 3		
	Romance, Op. 24, No. 9	GS	51 Piano Pieces from the Modern Repertoire
	Sunset, Op. 46, No. 8	BMC	From the Land of a Thousand Lakes
	Valse Mélancolique, Op. 54, No. 3		
SLAVENSKI, JOSIP (1865-1930)	Slowenisches Volkslied	Sch	The New Piano Book, Vol. III
STRAUSS, RICHARD (1864-1951)	Traumerei (Reverie), Op. 9, No. 4	GS GS	Published Separately 51 Piano Pieces from the Modern Repertoire
STRAVINSKY, IGOR (1882-)	Valse	Sch	The New Piano Book, Vol. III
SWANSON, HOWARD (1909-)	The Cuckoo (Scherzino)	L	Published Separately
TANSMAN, ALEXANDRE (1897-)	Four Impressions 1. Prelude 2. Invention 3. Nocturne 4. Burlesque	L	Four Impressions
	Four Piano Moods	L	Four Piano Moods
	From "Petite Suite" 3. Meditation 5. Plainte orientale 7. Scherzino	E	Petite Suite
TCHÉREPNINE, ALEXANDRE (1899-)	Bagatelles, Op. 5	I HC L	Bagatelles, Op. 5
	1. Allegro marciale 2. Con vivacita 3. Vivo 4. Lento con tristezza 5. Dolce 6. Allegro con spirito 7. Prestissimo 8. Allegro 9. Allegretto 10. Presto		
	Expressions, Op. 81	L	Expressions, Op. 81

Composer	Title	Publisher	Volume or Collection
TCHÉREPNINE, ALEXANDRE (cont.)	1. Entrance 3. Caprice 4. The Silly Story of the White Oxen 5. The Fleeting Vision 6. At the Fair 7. Barcarolle 8. Blind Man's Buff 9. At Dawn 10. Exit		
	From "Pour petits et grands", Set I 1. La Diligente	D	Pour petits et grands
	Set II 3. La Persévérante 5. Les Plaisirs du Toutou 6. La Belle au Bois Dormant		
	Intermezzo	Sch	The New Piano Book, Vol. II
	Petite Suite 1. Marche 2. Chant sans paroles 3. Berceuse 4. Scherzo 5. Badinage 6. Humoresque	D	Petite Suite
	Piéces sans titres (Pieces without Names) 1. Allegro 2. Allegretto 3. Moderato 4. Andantino 5. Allegro molto 6. Sostenuto 7. Allegretto 8. Impetuoso	D	Piéces sans titres
THOMSON, VIRGIL (1896-)	Piano Sonata, No. 4 1. Allegro 2. Adagio 3. Vivace	EV	Published Separately
TOCH, ERNST (1887-)	Dance for Ruth (From "Tanz und Spiel- stücken", Op. 40)	Sch	The New Piano Book, Vol. II
TURINA, JOAQUIN (1882-1949)	At the Shoemakers 1. Hans Sachs 2. The Marquise's Silken Slippers 3. The Peasant's Boots	Sch	At the Shoemakers

Composer	Title	Publisher	Volume or Collection

TURINA, JOAQUIN (cont.)	4. Greek Sandals
	5. The Shoes of the
	   Ballet Dancer
	6. The Dainty Shoes of
	   Her Ladyship
	7. Shoes of a Toreador		

	Miniatures 1. Out for a Walk 2. Soldiers Are Coming 3. The Village is Asleep 4. Dawn 5. The Market Place 6. Duo sentimental 7. The Festival 8. The Return	Sch	Miniatures
	The Circus 1. Fanfare 2. Jugglers 3. Equestrienne 4. The Trained Dog 5. Clowns 6. Trapeze Artists	Sch	The Circus
VILLA-LOBOS, HEITOR (1887-1960)	Alnilam (No. 2 from "The Three Maries")	CF	Masters of Our Day
	Alnitah (No. 1 from "The Three Maries")		
	Five Pieces, Album VII 1. In My Backyard 2. Go, Pumpkin 3. Let's Go, Maruca 4. The Little Doves 5. Round the Circle	MP	Five Pieces on Children's Folk Tunes of Brazil, Album 7
	From "Guia Prático" Album IX 2. Little Dove, Tiny Dove 4. The Old Woman That Had Nine Daughters	VL	Guia Prático, Album 9
	Pierrette's Hands	VL M	Carnaval Das Criancas Brasileiras Published Separately

KEY TO PUBLISHERS

A	Augener & Company, London (Galaxy Music Corporation)
ABR	Associated Board of the Royal Schools of Music, London (Mills Music, Inc.)
AME	American Music Edition, 263 E. 7th St., New York, N. Y. 10009
AMP	Associated Music Publishers, Inc., One W. 47th St., New York 36, N. Y
AX	Axelrod (Shawnee Press, Delaware Water Gap, Pa.)
B	Belwin, Inc., Rockville Centre, L. I., N. Y.
Ba	Barry, Buenos Aires (Boosey and Hawkes)
BB	Broude Brothers, 56 W. 45th St., New York 36, N. Y.
BH	Boosey and Hawkes, Inc., Oceanside, N. Y.
BMC	Boston Music Company, 116 Boylston St., Boston, Mass.
C	Chester Ltd., London (M. Baron Co., P. O. Box 149, Oyster Bay, N. Y. 11771)
Ce	Century Music Publishing Co., 39 W. 60th St., New York 23, N. Y.
CF	Carl Fischer, Inc., 56-62 Cooper Square, New York, N. Y. 10003
CO	Consolidated Music Publishers, Inc., 240 W. 55th St., New York 19, N. Y.
D	Durand, Paris (Elkan-Vogel Co.)
Do	Doblinger, Vienna (Associated Music Publishers)
E	Eschig, Paris (Associated Music Publishers)
EAM	Editorial Argentina de Musica (Southern Music Publishing Co., Inc.)
ECI	Editorial Cooperativa Interamericana de Compositores, Montevido, Uruguay (Peer International Corp.)
ECS	E. C. Schirmer Music Co., 600 Washington St., Boston 11, Mass.
EHM	Edwin H. Morris & Co., Inc., 31 W. 54th St., New York 19, N. Y.
EV	Elkan-Vogel Company, 1716 Sansom St., Philadelphia 3, Pa.
G	Galaxy Music Corporation, 2121 Broadway, New York 23, N. Y.
GS	G. Schirmer, Inc., 609 Fifth Avenue, New York 17, N. Y.
H	Hinrichsen Edition (C. F. Peters Corp.)
HC	Heugel & Cie, London (Theodore Presser Co.)
He	Heritage Music Publications, Inc., (Century Music Co.)
Ho	Charles Homeyer & Co., Inc., 156 Boylston St., Boston, Mass.
I	International Music Co., 509 Fifth Ave., New York 17, N. Y.
JF	J. Fischer & Bro., Harristown Road, Glen Rock, N. J.
K	Edwin F. Kalmus, P. O. Box 47, Huntington Station, L. I., N. Y. 11748
L	Leeds Music Corp., 332 W. 48th St., New York 36, N. Y.
Le	Leduc, Paris (M. Baron Co., P. O. Box 149, Oyster Bay, L. I., N. Y.)
M	Edward B. Marks Music Corp., 136 W. 52nd St., New York 19, N. Y.
MM	Mills Music, Inc., 1619 Broadway, New York, N. Y. 10019
MMC	Mercury Music Corp., (Theodore Presser Co.)
MMI	Merion Music Inc., (Theodore Presser Co.)
MP	Music Press (Theodore Presser Co.)
NV	Nagels Verlag (Associated Music Publishers)
O	Omega Music Edition, 19 W. 44th St., New York 18, N. Y.
OX	Oxford University Press, Inc., 417 Fifth Ave., New York 16, N. Y.
PAU	Pan American Union, Washington, D. C. (Peer Internation)
P	C. F. Peters Corp., 373 Park Ave., South, New York 16, N. Y.
PI	Peer International Corp., 1619 Broadway, New York, N. Y. 10019
PMP	Polish Music Publications, Cracow (Edward B. Marks)
PP	Paterson's Publications Ltd., London (Carl Fischer, Inc.)
R	Ricordi & Co., Milan (Franco Colombo Inc., 16 West 61st St., New York 23, N. Y.)
S	Salabert, Inc. (Franco Colombo, Inc., 16 West 61st St., New York 23, N. Y.)
Sch	Schott & Co., London, Brussels (Associated Music Publishers)

SG	Shroeder & Gunther (Associated Music Publishers)
So	Southern Music Publishing Co., 1619 Broadway, New York, N. Y. 10019
SS	Simon & Schuster, 630 Fifth Ave., New York 20, N. Y.
SU	Summy-Birchard Co., Evanston, Ill.
TP	Theodore Presser Co., Presser Place, Bryn Mawr, Pa.
U	Universal Music Co., (Theodore Presser Co.)
UME	Union Musical Espanola (Associated Music Publishers)
W	Willis Music Co., 440 Main St., P. O. Box 1758, Cincinnati 2, Ohio
Wo	B. F. Wood, Inc., (Century Music Co.)
WR	Winthrop Rogers Edition, London (Boosey and Hawkes)
VL	Villa-Lobos Music Corp., (Consolidated Music Publishers)

INDEX TO COMPOSERS

183